OUR KID EATS EVERYTHING!

NEELANJANA SINGH

With special inputs from Purnima Gupta

hachette
INDIA

First published in India in 2015 by Hachette India
(Registered name: Hachette Book Publishing India Pvt. Ltd)
An Hachette UK company
www.hachetteindia.com
SRD

ISBN 978-93-5009-928-5

Hachette Book Publishing India Pvt. Ltd
4th & 5th Floors, Corporate Centre
Plot No. 94, Sector 44, Gurgaon 122003, India

Typeset in Sabon LT Std 10.5/16.3 by
Eleven Arts, New Delhi

Printed and bound in India by
Manipal Technologies Limited, Manipal

FSC www.fsc.org
MIX
Paper from responsible sources
FSC™ C104740

OUR KID EATS EVERYTHING!

Neelanjana Singh is a well-known nutritionist with over 30 years of extensive experience in the field of nutrition. Over the years, she has worked at AIIMS, Sitaram Bharatiya Research Institute and the Diabetes Foundation. She currently consults at PSRI Hospital, New Delhi, and the Heinz Nutri Life Clinic, New Delhi, which offers free consultancy. Neelanjana has also taught Nutrition at the University of Delhi for more than seven years.

Neelanjana has been a weekly health columnist for *The Indian Express* for over three years and regularly contributes to several national dailies such as *The Hindustan Times*, *Mail Today* and *The Pioneer* on matters related to diet and health. In the past, she has run a free health portal for several years, which featured some of India's leading medical experts offering free advice. She has also been associated with the WHO as part of their committees and projects on nutrition and health. She serves on the advisory board of some of the top websites on health and nutrition, including *BabyCentre*. Neelanjana is the Joint Secretary of the Indian Dietetics Association, Delhi Chapter. She is also a Registered Dietician and a Certified Diabetes Educator.

Neelanjana believes that eating right is the best investment for good health that one can make for both the present and the future.

To my mother Prema from whom I learnt
my real lessons in nutrition
and
to my daughter, Richa, who gave me a chance
to practise that learning

Contents

FOREWORD

We all realize that nutrition is an integral part of a healthy lifestyle and we must eat right for good physical, mental and emotional health. We need guidance about food because it has been said, 'You become what you eat.' Be it in the areas of child, adolescent, adult or geriatric health, we need advice on what we eat.

Many of us do try to imbibe good eating habits and put in efforts to adopt a healthy lifestyle. but the challenges posed by long and erratic working hours, a sedentary lifestyle and many ready-to-eat options have led to a serious threat to our health. In recent years, with the increasing obsession with weight, many of us are seeking help to keep our BMI in the normal range. The ever-increasing effort to conform to a particular body image has resulted in a growing problem, evident in eating disorders, especially among teenagers and young women.

The Internet is the new answer to many of our problems. Many of us depend on search engines to answer our queries. While the Internet can help gather information about the right food, the right quantity and the right method to cook, we can get lost in this ocean of information. If we search for a 'healthy diet' we will get about 136,000,000 results on Google and 24,142 papers on PubMed (peer-reviewed medical literature). A search for obesity will show 22,400,000 results on Google and 19,1696 papers on PubMed. For weight loss, we will find 422,000,000 results on Google and 95,014 papers on PubMed. If that isn't information overload, what is? Social media sites are another source of information. On one click we can get so many tips that we can get confused. So how does one make sense of all this available information?

Here is a book which simplifies food with essential and crucial information about healthy eating. It demystifies and simplifies all dietary issues. Neelanjana Singh has brought her knowledge and decades of experience to create a wonderful and very useful book for parents concerned about a healthy diet for their children.

This book is a complete guide on nutrition for children, with tips for working parents, suggestions on how to make food interesting, dietary advice covering children's meals and the balance of dietary components.

What makes this book unique is the novel approach of the author. She has dwelt on the basics we all need to know and many books on the subject tend to ignore. We are given valuable insight into how to select raw food of high quality and the right methods of washing, storage and cooking as well as the ideal type of cookware. Instead of categorizing food as per the standard three-times-a-day plan, she has given a broader perspective of each food type and how it needs to be prepared to meet nutritional requirements. Each food group, right from water and beverages to oils, grains, nuts and lentils, is addressed separately according to nutritive value and required intake.

Being a paediatrician, I was delighted to read about the possible ways to persuade toddlers and young children to eat items on their list of 'not-so-desirable' foods, and actually get them to ask for them.

In this era of ever-growing lifestyle diseases, this book is a remarkable contribution to help society and I congratulate the author on her endeavour.

As George Bernard Shaw said, 'There is no sincerer love than the love of food', so all of you food lovers, happy reading!

Prof. Anupam Sibal
Group Medical Director, Apollo Hospitals Group
Senior Consultant Paediatric Gastroenterologist and Hepatologist, Indraprastha Apollo Hospitals
Adjunct Professor of Paediatrics, School of Medicine, University of Queensland, Brisbane, Australia

We are guilty of many errors and many faults, but our worst crime is abandoning the children, neglecting the fountain of life. Many of the things we need can wait. The child cannot. Right now is the time his bones are being formed, his blood is being made, and his senses are being developed. To him we cannot answer 'Tomorrow,' his name is today.

Gabriela Mistral, Nobel Laureate

Introduction

It's 7 am and the school bus will soon arrive. Your kids have just enough time to get dressed, gulp down a glass of milk and head out. Breakfast? No chance. They'd rather spend those extra few minutes on sprucing up their hair.

At lunchtime, your child insists that she's not hungry and leaves her plate untouched. Half an hour later, you find her munching on a bag of chips.

Your teenage son wants to follow the Zero Carb diet as he is putting on weight. He has heard that this is an effective way to lose weight quickly, but you worry that he is not eating all the foods that are important for his growth.

As a parent, you are bound to confront at least one of these situations more often than you would like. I assure you that there are ways out, which are easier and healthier than you imagine.

Over the years, as a practising nutrition consultant, I

have come to realize that in addition to prescribing the right diet, I spend a great deal of time trying to help my patients and clients to incorporate the suggested changes into their routine and implement them. When such is the case with knowledgeable and responsible adults, you can only imagine (and, as a parent, you would only know better!) how difficult it is to get children to eat right.

Nearly all children, at one time or another, seem to possess a unique 'gene' that makes them screw up their noses at the mere sight of healthy food, leaving parents exasperated!

Eating right is becoming an increasingly complicated and preoccupying issue for everyone, but even more so in the case of children. The good part is that there is no dearth of detailed information available about foods and nutrients, but the bad part is that often this information may not be of much use because it is either too complex to decipher or contradicts everything that you have thus far read and subscribed to.

Thanks to the people of my ilk, eating right has also become all about making sure you do no 'wrong'. If you are to eat right, you must follow one of the many rigorous diets doing the rounds, the rules of which serve to kill the joy of eating. Unfortunately, our modern-day encyclopaedia, Google, can never be consulted enough. When on a mission to get your children to eat right, you will have to learn to wade through the millions of search results, not knowing which ones are worth your time. Not only is it a task to bring traditional wisdom and new scientific knowledge into the same kitchen, you are constantly concerned about whether or not these coveted or recommended food items will appeal to your child's fussy palate.

Attractive advertisements for all kinds of unhealthy foods and suspiciously large portion sizes continue to play havoc with the health of our children. With easier and greater access to the not-so-healthy foods, children are becoming 'decision makers' about what they eat, and it is only very rarely that they go for the good stuff. At the same time, it is believed that being healthy is synonymous with following one of the fad diets in vogue. At the outset, I would urge you to dispel those beliefs.

Here is a book that tells you why it is of the utmost importance to feed your children wisely yet let them enjoy their food. All of this is possible and easy to implement without your suffering any kind of stress or guilt. It is just a matter of habit and a little mindfulness towards what our children eat. Healthy eating can help to increase children's levels of energy, sharpen their minds and even stabilize their moods. By encouraging healthy eating habits right from the beginning, you can make a lifelong impact on your children's relationship with food and give them the best opportunity to grow into healthy adults.

Did you know that a one-year-old child should be consuming all the same food groups that an adult needs? The basic principles guiding healthy eating are the same for adults and children, but the latter have specific nutritional needs for you to consider. This book aims to update you on the nutritional requirements of children, alert you to the pitfalls in the process of ensuring a balanced and appropriate diet for your child, and show the way to healthy eating.

In this book, I have tried to recreate simple and delicious food with relatively uncomplicated cooking methods and ingredients that are easy to procure, so that you can prepare the healthiest and tastiest meals for your child.

With an overview of the various food groups, and with practical tips gathered, tried and tested over the years, this book may make up for the wisdom of the elders who may be absent in the prevalent nuclear family setup. And, of course, it will also work as a stand-by for a personal dietician!

Our Kid Eats Everything addresses the most relevant issues that plague modern-day living by examining them under the lens of food and nutrition. Above all, it attempts to resolve these issues in a fuss-free and practical manner.

I do hope this book proves to be an indispensable reference guide for parents who would like to see their children smile at the sight of home-cooked food!

After all, the best and easiest way to stay healthy is to be enticed by a simple and yummy dish.

Here's to happy, healthy young people!

SECTION 1

NOW IS THE TIME

[1]

Eat Right from the First Bite

I empathize with all the young parents of today. They sure do have it tough as they live in the era of information overload, especially when it comes to nutrition. Gigabytes of information are available because people are hungrily looking for ways and means to improve their family's health and fitness. Their eagerness to eat right and feed their family right is evident, yet it is difficult to translate that keenness into reasonable everyday practice. A knowledgeable parent may, for instance, avoid serving the child greasy stuffed parathas for breakfast, but might replace it with a packaged cereal that is actually loaded with sugar and is in no way better.

Most of my clients come to me with queries related to their children's addiction to junk food, and their lack of time and inclination to eat breakfast early in the morning. A harried young mother once asked me if she was being a helicopter mom because she was worried about her son not eating broccoli and her daughter hating dal, and both demanding pasta at least four times a week. I told her to take it easy because there are enough ways to deal with fussy eaters. As for broccoli, there are plenty of wonderful substitutes, while dal can be incorporated into such unique recipes that your child will never guess that she is actually eating lentils! As far as their demand for pasta goes, it is acceptable to eat it often enough as long as it is *one* of the items of the meal (among salads, fruits and nuts) and not the whole meal itself.

It is important to address such concerns not only on the macro level but also on the micro level of every meal, because it is the growing-up years that are the foundation of adult health. Children from age one onwards grow taller and heavier till they reach adolescence – at a whopping rate of about 2–2.3kg every year for weight and 2–3 inches for height.

Besides growing, the body changes structurally, too. Bones are deposited with minerals to provide strength and density. The principal determinant of bone health can be judged by the peak bone mass. If you help your children achieve a good peak bone mass, it works as a health insurance, and the insult and loss of bone that will happen later on in life will be well compensated for. Peak bone mass development takes place during these growing years and, as a nutritionist, I cannot overemphasize that this is the window of opportunity every parent should make the most of. The irony is that this also happens to be the time when kids tend to be most carefree and consume food that has low calcium worth. Such neglect increases the risk of bone loss and fractures later in life. By the time one realizes one's follies and begins to make amends, calcium absorption in the body slows down and even mega doses of calcium will not help!

With regard to fat cells, too, childhood is the time to pay heed. It is during the growing-up years that fat cells increase in number and size due to faulty eating practices. Once the extra fat cells have been formed, they stay. All efforts to reduce weight can only reduce the size of the fat cells but not the number! This is why the problems of obesity and faulty eating have to be addressed right at the start.

We do know that childhood is the critical time in human development. Any neglect at this stage may cause more or less permanent damage and is difficult to rectify. Children from families with a history of chronic diseases need special attention as their diet can influence and even offset the effect of their genes. Tastes and eating habits developed in the early years tend to stay with children. Preferences for certain food items are established early in life and usually become set by the time the child is 11 years old. Once established, these preferences continue into adulthood. My own experience has confirmed this. I always thought that my children weren't eating enough of the right diet. Every now and then, they would express dissatisfaction with home-cooked food and demand chips and pizza. But it was quite an unexpected situation that made me realize that their eating habits were, in fact, excellent. They went on a holiday to visit their cousin, a young bachelor who lived alone and ate out almost all the time. I feared that my children would eagerly take to that lifestyle. But when they got to his apartment, they were amazed to find that his fridge was bereft of fruits, veggies, eggs and milk. They insisted on making a late-night trip to the supermarket so that they could at least eat a hearty breakfast the next morning. They had already rejected their cousin's suggestion of going to a nearby restaurant for breakfast. They wanted their egg, fruit and glass of milk. And, much to my surprise, throughout their stay, my kids made sure that they got their daily quota of fruits, veggies and milk. Although there was no one to monitor them, and in the face of complete freedom, the eating habits that had been inculcated in them all through their childhood came to their rescue. Now I am confident that even when they move out to study or to work, they will make sure that they eat the right things. Such is the power of childhood habits. Once formed, they are not easy to break! Remember to use this to your advantage.

A childhood dominated by sugary and greasy food usually leads to an adult who has a sweet tooth and likes fried munchies. This is why I recommend that children be helped early on to develop a taste for fresh, natural and varied foods. If the parents themselves are picky about the fruits that they eat, then is it surprising that their children are fussy eaters, too? The best way for you to encourage healthy eating in your kids is to lead by example. Parents who are always dieting, or always talking negatively about their bodies, may cause these same downbeat feelings in their kids.

Parents, your Children Are Watching you!

Parents should view the childhood years (1–19 years) as their single window to influence food preferences. After all, it is for you to decide *what* to offer the child. Moreover, it is important to make note of the things that *we* do wrong so that we, too, can learn with our children. This book is meant to guide your choices as parents, too.

At times, well-meaning parents can also go wrong because even a healthy but repetitive diet can lead to a fussy grown-up. Variety spices up life and diets from age one onwards need to be varied and interesting.

With the world transforming into one big global village, it is a good idea to be open to new foods and tastes. Like all things in life, a little effort now can yield great dividends later. A healthy child is well worth the hard work and patience. After all, no parent would like to be responsible, in any way, for the many common preventable diseases caused in a large part by the food their child eats.

Stay the Course

The process of change in food habits involves many stages. The first stage is the greater awareness of facts and scientific information. To focus on the course and stick to it is the next step. It is at this second stage that most parents begin to falter and give up. I would like to remind you that it takes *multiple tries* for children to like and develop the taste for a new food! Never give up without the effort that such a change deserves.

A good way of getting children to eat right is to involve them in the processes of food preparation. I have noticed in my interactions with many children that it is the ones who participate in the buying of fruits and veggies or in preparing meals at home that tend to eat better than those who are totally disengaged from these processes. A positive relationship with food is learnt at this early stage. Under all circumstances, avoid using certain foods as a reward for finishing up meals. Non-food enticement, such as playing a game, getting a hug or a cuddle, or a book, should be used as encouragement.

THE BIG 5 OF FOOD PROBLEMS

There is hardly a parent who has not faced these situations.

1. **Your child refuses a food item – a crucial one like vegetables. Obviously, you cannot ignore this. Forcing the child to eat is not an option.** ***What should you do?***
2. **Your child finds home-cooked food boring and unappetizing. S/he has developed a taste for sugary and fried foods.** ***How should you respond?***
3. **Your child wants a beverage like a cola or packaged juice every time s/he is thirsty.** ***Should you give in?***
4. **Your child is never hungry at mealtimes. Soon afterwards, s/he starts rummaging for snacks in the pantry.** ***Is this acceptable if the snacks are healthy foods?***
5. **Your child eats mostly what the family eats but adds on lots of junk food.** ***Should you let this be?***

Along the way, these questions will be answered. To start with, don't force-feed your child. Avoid the 'clean your plate' dictum. The child should be allowed to recognize the 'fullness' signals of the body. If you force your child to override these signals early on in life, you are paving the way to future problems connected with food, including high blood pressure, high cholesterol and a fatty liver. Children should be given the space to experience the feeling of 'fullness' and to be able to say 'no' to food after a point. Avoid heaping food on your child's plate despite his or her protests.

Second, in many homes, children are allowed to be choosy about what they eat as one feels that it is better that the child eats *something* rather than stays hungry. Yielding to the demand for potato chips or cold drinks is the easy way out, but it can be detrimental in the long run. The child should definitely be given the freedom to decide *how much* he or she wants to eat, but you are responsible for *what* is offered to the child. *Do not let the child dictate* what she or he wants to eat, at least not most of the time. With patience, firmness and love, solutions to such issues can be found. Love for children should not be expressed as immediate gratification of their whims and fancies, and food should never be used as the reward. There may be times when your child may leave the entire meal untouched. Do not be perturbed! Stay calm. Take the food away from the table, but do not fall into the trap of offering an unhealthy food swap in order to tempt the child into eating *something*.

Prevention is the Answer

We all know that prevention is better than cure, and also that prevention is much easier than reversing disease or chronic problems. However, one may think that with medical advances, treating diseases has become easier. This is far from the truth.

In fact, it's shocking to see the prevalence of many of the so-called 'adult' diseases in children. The ground reality is that urban Indian children as young as five years are also suffering from high blood pressure! In Delhi, ten thousand school-going kids were part of a study conducted by AIIMS in 2013, which showed that as many as three to four per cent of the children were suffering from this condition.

Heart disease can very well begin in childhood. Plaques of fat are seen in children as young as seven years of age. Besides high blood pressure, raised cholesterol and blood sugar levels – earlier considered to be 'adult' diseases – are now found in children. Low calcium, Vitamin D and iron levels are affecting their overall well-being by making many lethargic, low on energy and on concentration, too.

A poor or inappropriate diet has long-lasting implications. It not only impairs growth but also has an impact on mental development. The effects of poor nutrition can be seen in the form of lowered mental capacity at age 10 or 11 when the damage actually occurred at a much earlier age of 2 or 3 years.

Had I not been a mother, I would never have realized how important (and just how difficult!) it is to get children to eat right. It is also fairly well established that mere prescriptions for healthy eating do not work for children. No child will start eating more vegetables and fruits if we were to elaborate on the detrimental effects of not doing so. Many books available today prescribe what is healthy, but this advice is not quite enough to put it to practical use. For instance, asking a child to eat leafy vegetables and broccoli is possible using certain 'soft' strategies.

Pairing a favourite food with a new food that you wish to introduce is one such way. Among my own clients, I find that children consume veggies only when their favourite sauce/dip is offered along with it. This pairing strategy has immense potential and works for many foods that children otherwise dislike.

With a little innovation, children can be made to relish foods that they shun. For instance, pumpkin, broccoli, beans and the like can all be incorporated in dishes such as *pav-bhaji*, *tikkis*, cakes and chutneys.

Lifestyle Challenges

Today, children – particularly those from affluent families – are being detected with serious problems such as a fatty liver, diabetes, high blood pressure, obesity and anaemia – all purely due to faulty food habits. Iron deficiency in children continues to affect them in more ways than one. Low energy levels are a manifestation of anaemia or low iron levels in the body. A shortened attention span and lowered learning ability is also an expression of iron deficiency in the child. The behaviour and moods of children are also affected by dietary deficiencies, including that of iron. Lifestyle diseases like obesity and diabetes are on the rise and can in a large part be attributed to unhealthy eating habits. All one needs to do is to make small, *meditated changes* in the right direction.

It is ironic but true that most urban families have more than enough to eat, yet malnutrition is becoming a real threat for their children. This is primarily because of the overconsumption of unhealthy foods, which deny the body several important nutrients. A recent World Bank report reveals that even in affluent families, only a small percentage of children between 6–24 months of age receive the recommended quantity and quality of food. I get to see many overweight kids with anaemia and low energy levels.

Moreover, most overweight children are likely to grow up to be overweight adults and carry the added risk of degenerative diseases. A study published in *Pediatrics* 2005, on the relationship of childhood Body Mass Index (BMI – an index of weight in relation to height – *see page* 15) to adult adiposity showed that overweight 2–5 year olds were four times more likely to grow up into obese adults.

Many of the problems that we are dealing with today exist because we are going through a phase that is dominated by the culture of eating out. When eating out often, the risk of falling into a trap of deficiencies and excesses is almost inevitable. With interesting experiments carried out with home-cooked food and making the best choice when eating out, one can get the best of both worlds.

Besides food and nutrition, physical activity is another crucial determinant of health in children. Ironically, a sedentary way of life has replaced the good old days of playing outdoors. Children eat in front of the TV, order meals over the Internet or the phone, and play but only on the screen. Let's face it, the pressure on our children to perform well academically has also gone up several folds. Which is why it's not surprising that there's little room for physical activity in a child's routine. Although our grandparents knew it all along, today we need evidence to support all our lifestyle decisions, so here it is. The cognitive benefit that accrues from physical activity actually compensates for the time spent away from studying. The review of literature on this subject indicates that participation in physical activity is positively related to academic performance. Is this not enough reason for us to allow our children to play a game of their choice for an hour in their 24-hour schedule? Rest assured that this will not compromise your child's academic performance but only enhance it!

The research on the right type and right amount of exercise continues to delve deeper for the perfect answers, but there are some things that we already know for certain. Staying active, even in moderate doses, offers great benefits. This could mean playing a sport, climbing stairs, walking or swimming. It all does add up! The role of the family in encouraging physical activity in their children is effective. Sixty minutes of daily physical activity is recommended for children in the 2008 *Physical Activity Guidelines for Americans,* and one can take that as a broad guideline. As playgrounds are shrinking, parents would do well to keep children engaged in physical activities that they enjoy. It is time to hide those TV remotes and limit screen time.

Science is now confirming something that we perhaps knew all along. Kids who engage in enjoyable physical activity are more inclined to make healthier food choices.

However, wrong eating habits and the lack of physical activity are not the only culprits. Our mindsets, too, play a significant role. In our culture, especially, chubby children are mistaken for 'cute' and 'healthy'. It is ingrained in us that a thin child is not a healthy child, for the thinness must be a marker of the *lack* of food. We should fret not over these thin children but over the chubby ones.

It is also crucial for parents to understand the difference between a thin healthy child and a thin malnourished one. Children tend to have a high metabolism level, which is why many kids remain thin despite eating the wrong kinds of food. But the tastes acquired at this stage will haunt them forever! As we age, our metabolism slows down and physical activity decreases, but the taste for fatty and sugary foods remains. As long as the child is thin but healthy, there is no reason to worry. In fact, it is the plump child that we should be concerned about. The University of Nebraska-Lincoln, US, reviewed 69 studies that were conducted worldwide between 1990 and 2012, involving children between 2 and 18 years. The review revealed that more than half the parents of overweight/obese children thought that their children were slimmer than they actually were. When I mentioned this study to my son, he was thrilled to remark that parents don't always know best!

A study titled 'Age-related Consequences of Childhood Obesity' by the University of Colorado Cancer Center, US, published in the journal *Gerontology* in March 2014, suggests that the earlier in life a child becomes obese, the earlier will be the onset of diseases such as diabetes, cardiovascular disease and a fatty liver.

So it would be worthwhile to regularly check the BMI of the child during visits to the paediatrician.

A 2014 European study with 16,220 children was undertaken at the University of Gothenburg, Sweden, in

BMI (BODY MASS INDEX) DECODED

This index is helpful in detecting problems of excess or deficiency of body fat. BMI reflects body fat percentage and is a useful tool that helps to categorize healthy and unhealthy weights.

Calculating the BMI of a child is a little different from that of an adult. In adults the fat percentage remains more or less constant whereas in children it is not so. The patterns of growth differ in girls and boys. The body fat percentage also varies at different stages of growth. Thus both the age and gender of the child are taken into account when calculating BMI for children. Weight-to-age percentiles are used to detect weight problems in children instead of a definite BMI figure used for adults. A BMI percentile too high or too low in childhood is associated with increased risk of ill health even later on in adulthood.

which parents were asked to estimate their child's weight status. One out of every two parents of overweight children felt that their child's weight was normal. Four of every 10 parents of the obese/overweight children were actually worried that their children may lose some weight! It is best to rely on objective scores rather than on your personal judgment on this matter!

Take a look at the charts on the following pages. In order to plot your child's weight–to–age percentile, find the age at the bottom of the chart and the weight on the left arm of the chart. Look at the colour shade where the two points meet and this will give you an idea of the child's weight status. If the child's weight-to-age percentile is above the 95th percentile, the child is obese. Between the 85th and 95th percentile the child is overweight and at risk of being obese.

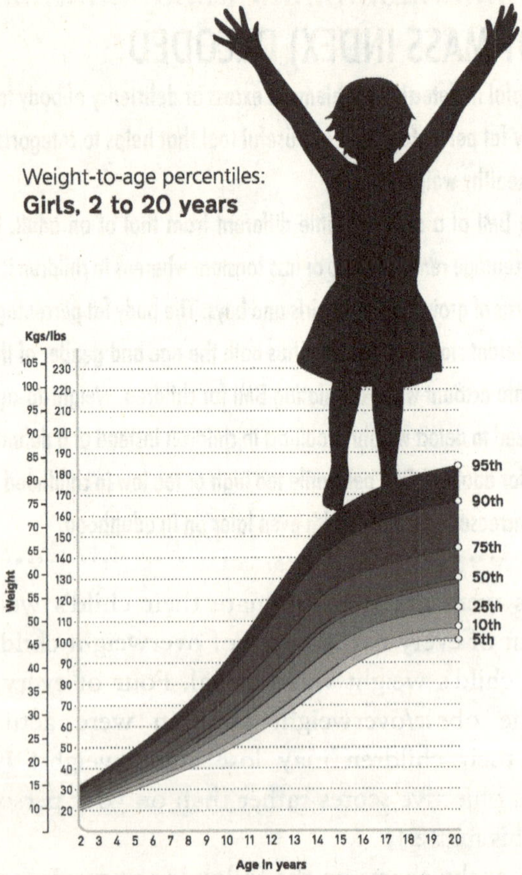

Adapted from the BMI tables of the Obesity Foundation of India

Weight-to-age BMI Chart

BMI	Recommended Classification
5th percentile or less	Underweight
5th to 85th percentile	Healthy weight
85th to 95th percentile	Overweight
95th percentile and above	Obesity

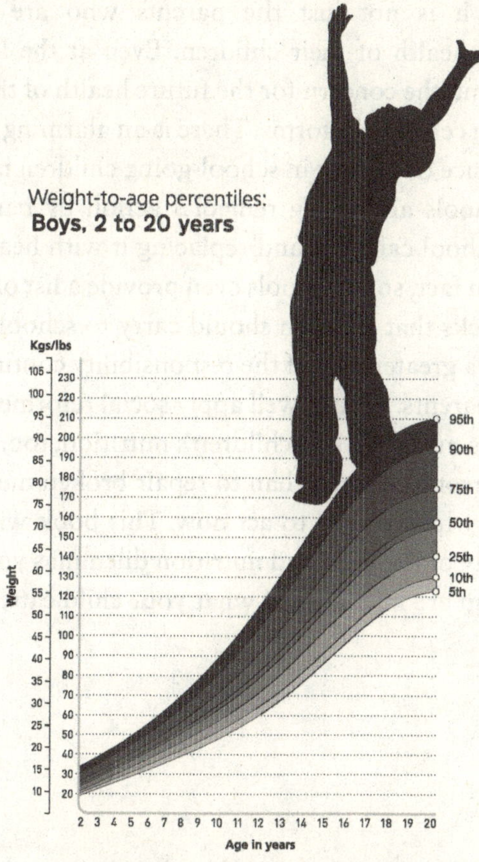

Adapted from BMI tables of Obesity Foundation of India

Researchers have been on the lookout for sure-shot methods of catching health problems in children as early as possible. One such way of screening is the measurement of waist circumference. It is being realized that measuring the waist size of children helps to warn against early signs of obesity and related problems.

Today, it is not just the parents who are concerned about the health of their children. Even at the level of the government, the concern for the future health of the nation is evident on certain platforms. There is an alarming increase in the incidence of obesity in school-going children in the cities. Many schools are taking remedial action by banning junk food in school canteens and replacing it with healthier food options. In fact, some schools even provide a list of nutritious foods/snacks that children should carry to school. However, I feel that a greater part of the responsibility continues to rest with the parents. We can well apply social reformer Frederick Douglass's maxim to our children's nutrition, too: 'It is easier to build strong children than to repair broken men.'

This is why we need to act now. This book will help you solve many of the food and nutrition dilemmas you may face so that you are in charge of what your child eats.

SECTION 2
GETTING TO KNOW FOOD

[2]

Meet the Food Families

The secret of a healthy diet really lies in the right foods taken in appropriate amounts. Very often, I come across parents who worry that all their attempts at offering healthy food choices seem to have no impact on their children as they continue to prefer fried, sugary things over the healthier options.

Dr Lucy Cooke of University College London, UK, says, '(Our) research shows clearly that a programme of introducing children to unfamiliar foods regularly and over a sustained period will lead to greater familiarity and eventually enjoyment of these foods – so for the best results, it is worth persisting using this structured approach.'

How does one go about ensuring a healthy diet for the future generation? One simple approach would be to include all the foods from the various food groups in the right amounts, based on age, gender and activity levels.

There are many ways to classify foods. Currently, the most popular way is the classification into six groups: Dairy; Vegetables and Fruits; Grains/Cereals; Pulses/Meat, Fats, Oils, Nuts and Seeds; and Sugar and Honey. Choosing the right proportions from each of the food groups is the first step towards achieving a balanced diet for your child.

Another way of grouping foods is based on the functions they perform:

- ***Energy providing foods:*** Carbohydrates and fats
- ***Body-building foods:*** Proteins and minerals
- ***Protective foods:*** Vitamins and minerals
- ***Regulatory foods:*** Water and roughage

Yet another classification of food is based on its nutrients: Water, Roughage, Carbohydrates, Fats, Proteins, Vitamins and Minerals.

The purpose of all these classifications is the same: to understand and ensure appropriate nutrients for the body, based on its needs. I have also devised my unique way of ensuring healthy eating, which is the 20/20 Action Plan (*see Chapter 17*).

Other Dimensions of Food

The truth is that food offers more than just the sum of the nutrients mentioned earlier. Even the non-nutrient components have tremendous value. There are so many non-nutrient components in food – natural pigments and colours, fibre, aroma and taste, for instance – that all add up for our children's well-being. This is the reason why a pill can never ever replace food. Pills should be used only to supplement a diet that is deficient in certain nutrients, or in some situations, to take care of the body's enhanced needs that are not achievable with the diet alone.

Three papers published in the *Annals of Internal Medicine*, US, in 2013 have reaffirmed that the healthiest approach is to obtain your vitamins from food and not from supplements. Food remains the best source of nutrients. Supplements are useful only to replenish deficient nutrients. They can be used for children who are on restrictive diets or for those with food allergies. It is best to avoid routine multivitamin-mineral use as this carries its own set of problems.

Our forefathers always knew that there is more to food than just nutrients. That is why our parents and grandparents laid so much emphasis on *how* to eat – in a calm, relaxed environment – for which we now have scientific evidence. I have to confess that when I started out as a nutritionist, I was more or less convinced that healthy eating was primarily about the nutritive worth of the diet. With years of experience, I have realized that this is far from the truth. Apart from counting calories and nutrients, it is *how* we eat that is of equal importance. In order to be attuned to the signals of satiety and fullness that our body emits, we ought to switch off distractions such as the TV and mobiles while eating.

I would like to direct your attention to a disturbing trend unfolding around us. Fewer parents have meals with their children these days. The practice of eating meals together as a family has a positive impact on the well-being of the child. Studies show that children and adolescents who grow up eating meals with their families perform better academically and are less likely to engage in health-risking behaviours such as smoking and drinking alcohol. They are also less prone to eating disorders and other psychiatric problems.

Watching TV while eating does not allow children to focus on chewing, and it also deters them from enjoying the meal to the fullest. Listening to hunger-fullness signals is equally crucial for their healthy growth and fitness. When one savours the food in the mouth while eating slowly and chewing mindfully, there is bound to be greater satisfaction at the end of the meal. Try to get children to enjoy the entire experience of eating – the smell, colour, flavour, touch and sound. Eating with all the five senses leads to satisfaction and satiety, and curbs one's tendency to overeat.

Psychological contentment with the meal is as important as its nutritive content. It is not surprising that the presentation of food is of great value when feeding children. Children are known to eat with their eyes. I can vouch for the fact that the visual appeal of food can alter your child's attitude towards the food. For instance, a whole fruit may not be attractive for the child, but the same fruit chopped into small pieces and threaded on a skewer/toothpick can make all the difference! Cooking in a way that retains and enhances flavours, and presenting food so that it is appealing are all easily learned skills.

At all meals and in-betweens, encourage a liking for natural flavours – especially of fresh fruit, veggies, yogurt, milk, water and egg – so that such tastes become the preferred ones. Again, preparing food in a way that keeps its natural flavours is crucial so that everything is not an over-spiced, similar-tasting blob.

The Secret of Food Families

The definition of a good diet emphasises the need to incorporate all the food groups or families in the correct proportions. Here's an overview of the six food families.

MILK AND MILK PRODUCTS FAMILY

I am certain that there are very many kids who, like me, would rather start the day with a glass of milk in the time-tested way than with any other food item. This food makes perfect sense nutritionally and is also a practical breakfast item. Unfortunately, there is a great deal of controversy regarding the consumption of animal milk. Let's find out what the concerns really are.

WHAT ARE THE WORRIES REGARDING MILK?

Concern #1

Use of hormones (oxytocin) and drugs (antibiotics) given to cattle.

This kind of apprehension is valid for all kinds of animal foods. Vegetarian foodstuffs also have their own set of problems related to the use of synthetic

dyes, ripening agents, colours and other adulterants. The solution to such problems lies in increasing public awareness and enforcing stricter laws, and not in negating the good effects of milk. Nonetheless, opting for established, reputed brands does offer the advantage of better quality products.

Concern #2

Why do humans drink animal milk?

Why does the human child need to drink animal milk, when it seems to be the norm of nature that every animal only drinks the milk of its own species? Humans have many characteristics that set them apart from all other animal species and thus the dissimilarities from other species. One of them is knowing what's good for us – and milk is!

Concern #3

Three or more glasses of milk harm the body.

A recent study by Swedish scientists, published in 2014 in the *British Medical Journal*, seems to convey that consuming three or more glasses of milk harms the body by causing brittleness in bones and increased risk of other diseases.

As with all such studies, the jury is still out. In fact, many leading scientists have questioned several aspects of the study. I believe that there is no reason to be alarmed by the recent studies on milk consumption.

Milk is one of the best sources of protein in the diet. For one, protein deficiency is prevalent in India where the majority of the population is vegetarian, unlike in western countries (where this study was conducted). Secondly, almost all foods in those countries – juices, cereals and so on – are fortified with calcium and Vitamin D. For the Indian population, milk is a significant source of calcium and Vitamin D as well.

Interestingly, the study in question is only concerned with the regular intake of 3 or more glasses of milk in a day, which in the first place is an uncommon practice in India.

It is worthwhile to note that Ayurveda, a great body of knowledge in practice in India for thousands of years, has nothing but good things to say about the consumption of milk. Secondly, the Indian subcontinent has its own indigenous breed of cattle, and the properties and benefits of this milk are unique.

Finally, it is important to consume a balanced diet including all the food groups. If any one kind of food or food group is taken in excess, it certainly means that the other groups will get neglected (resulting in a deficiency).

Until there is further evidence on the matter, especially in the Indian context, I strongly recommend that children must consume 2–3 glasses milk/milk products as part of a balanced diet.

Is Dairy Essential for Children?

In one word, yes. It is an excellent source of vitamins (A, D, B_1, B_2 and B_{12}) and minerals, particularly calcium. This is especially important for children and adolescents (a period of growth when most nutritional neglect may occur). Incidentally, mineral absorption peaks during adolescence and, once ignored, this window of opportunity is missed forever.

Besides high-quality protein, milk and other dairy products contain a special kind of fat known as conjugated linoleic acid (CLA), a biologically active chemical produced in the intestines of animals. CLA has shown promise in reducing food allergy reactions and obesity. It also has the potential to improve immunity.

For a growing body in need of sensible nutrition, dairy has no substitute and for reasons of sound nutrition, dairy should remain an integral part of the human diet. There is overwhelming evidence to show that consuming adequate amounts of calcium in foods such as cheese or yogurt throughout life may delay or minimize age-related bone loss, thereby decreasing the risk of osteoporosis and fractures later in life. Adequate calcium intake increases bone gain during the growth phase. A good bone balance can be achieved during childhood and teenage years only if borrowing from the bones is minimized and the daily calcium needs are met.

However, it is not uncommon to come across children who are averse to drinking milk and some others who just do not take to it. There are kids like my daughter who complained of a stomach-ache every morning when she drank a glass of milk before leaving for school. Back then, I mistook this as a ploy on her part to skip school, or to skip milk! It was after many years of this constant complaint that I swapped the glass of milk with a glass of lassi and she did not complain. She had obviously been suffering from some degree of lactose intolerance.

LACTOSE INTOLERANCE

When I meet clients who complain of symptoms such as cramps or bloating after drinking milk or consuming milk products, I think of lactose intolerance as a likely reason.

This is a very commonly discussed topic, yet there is not enough clarity on what it is. The level of intolerance to lactose – the sugar present in milk – can vary from person to person. The interesting part is that even

those individuals who are symptomatic (those who show one or the other symptoms of intolerance) can tolerate some amount of lactose in the diet. Total elimination of lactose is usually not necessary.

All you need to do is reduce the amount of lactose in the diet. This can be done by using foods that are derived from milk but have a lower lactose content than that of milk. Examples of lower lactose milk products are yogurt, buttermilk and cheese. The bacteria (usually a strain of lactobacillus) added in the process of cheese- and yogurt-making converts the lactose, which is a carbohydrate, into simpler forms that are easily digested by lactose intolerant persons as well. Otherwise, one could consume only small amounts of milk/dairy products at a time along with other lactose-free foods so that the load of lactose at that meal is minimal. Each person has a threshold dose below which they remain symptom-free. The intolerance occurs when the amount of lactose in one go tends to be large.

The milk sugar (lactose) is found in human, cow, buffalo, goat milk and their products. Whey (a byproduct of cheesemaking) is commonly added to foods such as breads, biscuits and muffins. Whey is rich in lactose and does add up to the total tally of lactose ingested in a day. Hidden lactose is found in non-dairy creamers, breads, cakes and cream soups. It is important to scrutinize labels to be aware of products containing lactose besides milk and its products. Casein, whey, galactose, skimmed milk powder/solids or milk sugar, all contain lactose. Foods with low lactose should have <1g lactose/100g of food. One glass (240 ml) of milk contains 12g lactose. Skimmed milk and full-cream milk contain the same amount of lactose.

The Committee on Nutrition of the American Academy of Pediatrics supports drinking milk even in areas of the world where the incidence of

lactose intolerance is high. The focus of our attention should be to make use of strategies to reduce the lactose content for those who are intolerant rather than to eliminate it completely. A negative calcium balance could occur in children due to severe restrictions on milk and its products.

Milk Products

Yogurt

Yogurt is a good option for lactose intolerant youngsters. Greek yogurt is a thicker and smoother version of regular yogurt. It has relatively less lactose and lower sugar content, whereas the protein content is higher than in regular yogurt. Yogurt has many advantages over milk.

1. *It's easier to digest than milk. It takes the stomach 60 minutes to break down animal milk but only 30 minutes for yogurt.*
2. *The calcium and phosphorous in curd are better assimilated by the body.*
3. *The levels of B vitamins are higher.*
4. *It can be consumed by lactose intolerant people.*
5. *It's easier to store at home for longer periods.*
6. *It contains beneficial bacteria. Once the good bacteria reach our gut, they also play a role in supporting the growth of other good bacteria and suppressing the bad ones.*
7. *It prevents many chronic diseases.*

Fermented foods such as yogurt help in acquiring the right microbiota (microbes in the gut). These bacteria aid the prevention and treatment of diarrhoea, and the prevention of fatty liver disease. Yogurt aids cholesterol reduction and weight management. It also eases Irritable Bowel symptoms.

For some kids, however, the aversion to milk and yogurt is so strong that it is worthwhile to look at other options in order to fulfil their nutritional requirements (more on this later in the chapter). But giving up dairy altogether in such cases is not an option, which is where the likes of paneer and cheese make an appearance.

PROBIOTICS

The idea of including good bacteria in the diet is not new! As early as 1908, Russian biologist Elie Metchnikoff, known as the father of probiotics, stated that 'taking a mixture of micro-organisms can improve health.'

The market for probiotics is expanding, but there is much confusion prevailing around it. Probiotics are *live* micro-organisms, which when administered in *adequate* amounts confer health benefits on the host. The word probiotic means 'advantageous bacteria'. Quite evidently, not all live micro-organisms can be labelled probiotic unless the benefit to the host has been established.

Humans are 'super organisms' as the human metabolism is the sum total of its own interaction along with that of the 500 species of microbes living in their gut. More than 100,000 billion bacteria thrive mainly in the colon. Current scientific evidence suggests that probiotic bacteria have a beneficial role in maintaining gut health and immunity. It is interesting to note that different strains of the same species of bacteria could play entirely differing roles in the human body.

A study published in June 2014 in the medical journal *Gut* shows the link between exercise and gut flora on the basis of research at University College Cork, Ireland, where the gut flora of rugby players was studied. The study showed that the players harboured more beneficial bacteria (those that reduced inflammation and obesity) than sedentary people. Here is more reason for children to be involved in sports and other physical activity!

Consuming probiotic yogurt on a regular basis reduces the uptake of environmental toxins by the body.

The home-set yogurt is extremely beneficial, but cannot be labelled a 'probiotic' unless the colony count and the bacteria species present in it are specified.

Paneer and Cheese

These are milk derivatives and can be substituted for milk. However, the fat content of these products makes calorie-conscious parents wary. This problem can be tackled by choosing wisely and controlling the portion.

Paneer or cottage cheese is a great favourite among north Indians. The kind that you get in the market, however, is usually prepared with full-cream milk and is thus high on fat. Paneer that is made with low-fat milk is healthier and can be incorporated into many recipes (see *Recipes*).

Cheese is a very handy food. Not all types of cheese are alike in terms of nutritive worth, particularly in terms of the fat content (which ranges between 20 per cent to 75 per cent). Ricotta, feta, cottage and light mozzarella are healthier choices since they have a lower fat content as opposed to Brie, Cheddar and cream cheese (which are quite high on fat levels). Edam has a moderate content of fat but its sodium content is quite high, which is why it should be used sparingly or occasionally. Cheese happens to be a good source of conjugated linoleic acid (CLA) and sphingolipids, which play a role in the prevention of cancers. Quite like milk, cheese is a good source of calcium, phosphorous, magnesium, Vitamin D, Vitamin B_{12} and zinc. Being high on protein, cheese provides satiety value and helps manage weight very effectively.

HOW MUCH MILK/DAIRY PRODUCTS SHOULD CHILDREN CONSUME?

2 to 3 servings of reduced, low-fat or no-fat dairy and its products (milk, cheese and yogurt) are essential for growth and development.

(1 serve of milk = 250ml = 1 cup)

45g cottage cheese (paneer) = 1 serve of milk

2 slices of cheese = 1 serve of milk

Note: There is no need to give low-fat or fat-free milk to children until the age of two years. Many parents who are enthusiastic about healthy eating start restricting fat a bit too early for children.

Going Vegan? Read This First!

A vegan diet is considered healthy as it is low in fat, particularly the saturated variety, and quite high on fibre. This plant-based diet has higher levels of antioxidants and phytochemicals present in it. It excludes all animal-derived foods, including meat, poultry, eggs, fish, milk and cheese.

However, a vegan diet is not advisable for children, unless there are allergy or intolerance concerns. Such a diet is low on Vitamin D, calcium, Vitamin B_{12}, iron and zinc, the lack of which can cause serious and lasting health concerns later in life. For one, Vitamin B_{12} deficiency can cause damage to the nervous system of the child. Moreover, the high fibre content of these diets tends to provide lower energy intake. Children have smaller stomachs and are likely to feel full sooner on vegan diets without reaching the required energy goal. The complete absence of all meat, milk and dairy products could compromise the growth and development of children, making it necessary to fulfil nutritional needs with supplemental and fortified foods.

VEGGIE AND FRUIT FAMILY

There are so many different diets in vogue that no two nutritionists seem to agree on anything. Some believe in fasting for health, others in high-protein diets and yet others support the macrobiotic diet. The only advice all nutritionists agree on is: 'Eat your vegetables and fruits and make sure you eat plenty of them'.

I had very different experiences with my two children while getting them to eat their quota of vegetables. When my son was a year old, he would eat every vegetable that

I prepared including pumpkin, spinach and beetroot, while my daughter refused to taste a morsel of food that resembled a veggie. After years of my sticking to the five-a-day rule for veggies, my daughter definitely eats many more vegetables than she used to. It is important not to give up, and to persist, because veggies are worth that effort.

Vegetables can be added to almost all foods: cereals, dals, pastas, chutneys and sauces. The strategy that worked with my children was 'disguising' vegetables in sauces and breads. My children love pesto, so I started making it at home using basil leaves. Gradually, I switched to using all other edible leaves in the sauce (instead of just basil) and that is how I made sure they got a portion of their veggie requirements.

Another sauce where I do sneak in some more veggies is the romesco. In this recipe, roasted red peppers, along with almonds/cashews, oil and vinegar are blended together. This sauce goes well with almost everything – fish, vegetables, and tofu (see *Recipes*).

Getting children to eat vegetables in the summer is especially tough. They screw up their noses at the mere mention of *lauki*, *tori* and *parwal*. We know that the summer vegetables are rich in water content and fibre. The high water content makes them easily digestible and the high fibre content provides the feeling of satiety and prevents overeating. Minerals such as sodium, potassium, magnesium and phosphorous – which get lost in sweat – are also present in these vegetables. These veggies, sadly, are not popular with kids.

DISGUISED DELICACIES

Here's how you can get your kids to eat summer veggies.

BOTTLE GOURD (*Lauki*): Make chilled soup with *moong* or *masoor* dal boiled with *lauki* and tomatoes, and served with cold pasta salad.

SNAKE GOURD (*Tori*): Slice thinly; dip in *besan* (gram flour) batter and shallow fry. You can do the same with *bhindi*. *Tori* or zucchini prepared in this way can be eaten with a yogurt dip. *Tori* could also be sliced thinly and sautéed in a pan with butter and herbs such as dill.

BABY SQUASH (*Tinda*): Mince finely and cook Chinese-style with chopped spring onions, ginger, garlic and green chillies. Add soya sauce. Serve with boiled rice.

IVY GOURD (*Kundru*): This curbs appetite and reduces blood sugar levels in diabetics. Shallow-fry thin slices on a *tawa* and sprinkle with tandoori masala.

AMARANTH (*Cholai saag*): You can use either the red or green type. Make rotis and spread with a paste of the cooked leaves. Serve the roti along with cheese/paneer and onions, like a Mexican quesadilla.

TENDER GREEN MANGO: Add to salads or dips. Protects against sunstroke.

PUMPKIN (*Kaddu*): Rich source of beta-carotene. Add to cake or muffin batter. Adds moisture and texture.

Note: Overcooking of vegetables of the gourd family mars their texture and makes us lose out on the subtle flavour and the much-valued water content, folic acid and Vitamin C.

Raw or Cooked?

Vegetables are valuable elements of our diet. The debate is about how it would be best to eat them – raw or cooked?

Do raw and cooked veggies affect the body differently? The answer is yes, cooking does alter the nutrient profile of food in many ways.

Consuming raw veggies has its set of pluses. They leave an alkaline ash in the body, which helps in the absorption of many nutrients. The carbohydrates in uncooked vegetables are absorbed slowly by the body, which is why they are good for diabetics and weight watchers.

When veggies are cooked, the heat-sensitive nutrients such as Vitamin B complex and Vitamin C are lost in the process. The heat of cooking can also destroy the beneficial enzymes present in the veggies. Cauliflower, broccoli, Brussels sprouts and garlic contain special anti-cancer enzymes, such as allinase. Overcooking inactivates this beneficial heat-sensitive enzyme. Food microwaved for only as many as 60 seconds destroys much of it. Which is why it makes a lot of sense to have some of these veggies raw.

Garlic is also best eaten raw, but make sure that you crush or cut the garlic cloves and let them stand for 10 minutes before eating it. This allows for the full activation of the beneficial enzymes in garlic.

Nevertheless, heating and cooking have their own set of benefits:

1. Cooking makes food safer by destroying harmful microbes.
2. It improves digestibility.
3. Vitamin A and lycopene (found in yellow and red vegetables) get converted into forms that are better utilized by the body. Thus, the availability of these nutrients goes up manifold.

So give your children a mix of both raw and cooked veggies, but avoid overcooking.

Overcooking, i.e., increasing the cooking time and temperature is not advisable as it leads to the formation of harmful products, such as AGE (advanced glycation end products), which are responsible for allergies, digestive disorders and accelerated ageing. This is particularly true of the dry methods of cooking such as grilling and roasting.

How Much is Enough?

Appetite varies from one person to another, so how do you figure out if your child is getting an adequately balanced amount of vegetables? Here is a quick way to check. Picture your child's plate and divide it into two equal halves. If one half of the plate is taken up by veggies, fruits and beans, then you are on the right track.

For practical purposes, ensure that your child eats at least three differently coloured plant foods every day (from among green, white, yellow/orange, blue/purple and red). The vegetables and fruits in our diet provide not only vitamins and minerals but also phytochemicals that help in the prevention of heart disease and certain cancers. The red colour of tomato and watermelon is the pigment lycopene, which is a phytochemical. Similarly, the orange pigment of sweet potatoes and pumpkin is another pigment of great value and so is the green colour of the many leaves that we consume. This is why all nutritionists recommend including a variety of differently coloured fruits and vegetables.

***MAKING THE MOST OF VEGGIES:** Wash and dry the leaves of cauliflower/carrots/radish on a muslin cloth or any absorbent material. Once dry, chop them into large pieces and microwave them until crisp. Cool and then crush to a fine powder. Add spices of your choice and use as a sprinkle on dals or vegetables.*

Fruits and vegetables have a lot in common. Both foods are rich in coloured pigments, water, vitamins and minerals. The other similarity is that both are good sources of fibre without being high on calories. The one difference between the two foods is how we eat them – fruits usually raw and veggies usually cooked. The two foods are interchangeable, if required, for practical reasons. The main emphasis should be on consuming the recommended five portions of fruits and vegetables every day.

DID YOU KNOW?

- **Eating many different types of fruits and veggies is better than eating those of the same colours all the time.**
- **Fruits and vegetables that look the best (read attractive) may not be the best in terms of nutrients. Apples that are used to produce cider (usually the least good-looking ones) have more of the beneficial chemical phloridzin (the enemy of viruses) than the glossy variants. The bruises on fruits and vegetables are indicative of higher levels of protective chemicals that the plant has produced as a defence mechanism, so picking the best-looking stock may not be the best bet!**

GRAINS/CEREALS FAMILY: OUR DIET'S BACKBONE

All over the world, from the earliest times, cereals have been the mainstay of the regular diet. What has changed is the way we consume them. Firstly, cereals have become more refined and processed to suit our modern tastes. Secondly, we have forgotten traditional grains like millets and have restricted ourselves mainly to wheat and rice. Until 50 years ago, in different regions of the country, many varieties of millets were used to make an assortment of dishes. Besides millets, there are a variety of whole grains which can be part of the everyday diet of our kids.

The Whole Grain Kernel

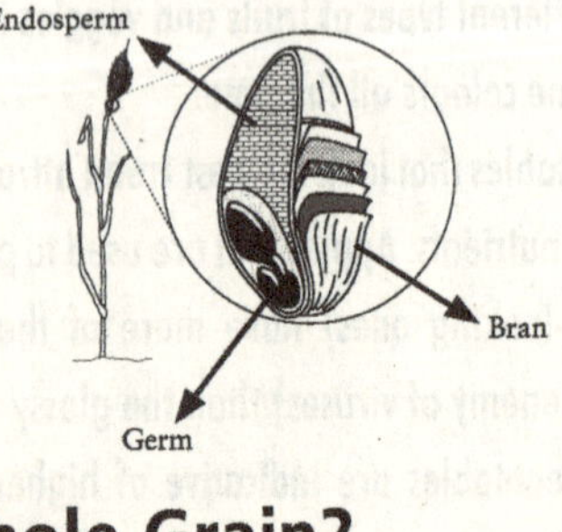

What Is a Whole Grain?

A whole grain is a grain that has its three essential parts intact:

BRAN: The outer shell, which is rich in fibre, Vitamin B complex and some minerals.

ENDOSPERM: The middle shell that contains carbohydrates and protein.
GERM: The inner shell that contains antioxidants, Vitamin E and B complex vitamins.
In refined flour, only the endosperm remains, which is mostly starch, bereft of vitamins or minerals.

Fibre, found in abundance in unprocessed or minimally processed cereals, offers many benefits, such as a reduced risk of heart disease, infectious and respiratory diseases and certain cancers.

Our children are getting accustomed to smooth, textured foods that they eat often as processed, packaged foods. Besides processing, the food industry has been adding taste stimulators/enhancers to foods, and it is no surprise that after eating such foods, kids find the regular home food lacking in taste! Once the taste buds are corrupted by highly salted and sugary food in the early years, natural foods will seem coarse and bland.

If you include a wide variety of minimally processed and natural foods in the early years of childhood, it will help to preserve the sensitivity of the taste buds. It would be ideal if children, in this age of processed foods, get initiated into eating some of the traditional grains as well. This may well be difficult. The one trick that seems to work well with kids is to give the food item an interesting and trendy name. This is how I have managed to get children to try traditional foods! Which is why a fancy name, such as 'lentil pilaaf' or 'lentil risotto', and some amount of innovative preparation have been effective in getting many kids to like *khichri*.

BREADS AND MORE

Breads are popular because they are tasty and convenient. Most of us believe that wholegrain bread is just as good a substitute for roti, but this is not true. The fibre content of breads is usually much lower than that of the wholegrain cereal flour. Usually, to make the bread soft and fluffy, a mix of whole grain and refined grain is used. You wlll notice this on the label. It is quite hard to find good bread that does not contain refined flours.

Moreover, almost all breads tend to have a much higher content of sodium as opposed to the traditional unleavened bread or roti. A single slice of bread could have as much as 230mg of sodium, which comes from the baking soda/ powder and the added salt. Plus, fats of different kinds are added in the bread-making process, which are not required while making a roti. It is, therefore, best to limit bread to one meal in a day.

Amongst cereal choices, different kinds of breads have seen a meteoric rise in popularity in the last decade or so. Different flours are being used to make breads. Here are some pointers to help you choose the right one:

WHOLEWHEAT/WHOLEGRAIN: This type of bread uses grain with the bran and germ intact. If the label mentions whole grain as the first ingredient, go for it.
RYE: A grain popular in Europe. The bread is dense and dark with a strong flavour. Makes for a healthy option.
MULTIGRAIN: A combination of different grains are used, but not necessarily whole grains. Usually contains more fibre than white bread.
OATMEAL: Oats contain beta-glucans that have cholesterol-lowering properties.

SOURDOUGH: Contains lactobacillus culture and yeast. Fermented and easy to digest.

Tips on Buying Bread

When buying bread, the following indicators will keep you on the right track:

- **The label should list wholewheat/wholemeal flour as its first ingredient.**
- **Don't be misled by the name 'enriched flour', which is actually the same as 'refined flour'.**
- **The presence of caramel in the ingredients indicates that the colour of the bread is not from the wholegrain component.**
- **Try and look for bread with these specifications: 2g fibre per slice, sodium content <200mg per slice, saturated fat <500mg per slice and zero trans fats.**

The Daily Roti

Roti can be of varied kinds. It can be made with wheat flour, jowar (sorghum), bajra (spiked millet), multigrain flour and also with different combinations of the same. One can add *besan or* soya flour, or knead in some *methi*, spinach, mint or even seeds to enhance its nutritive worth. It is good to eat a variety of grains and have different combinations. One such mix for rotis would be a cereal–pulse combo – a grain such as barley/wheat mixed along with soya/any dal flour.

Rice

Rice, the most widely consumed grain, is classified based on the size of the grain. Short grains, in general, have more complex carbohydrates and, therefore, are healthier for kids unless in special circumstances when one wants to restrict carbohydrates. The choice of short- or long-grain rice depends upon the kind of dish one wants to prepare. In general, the long grains are firmer and drier when cooked while the short grains tend to be sticky and chewy due to the extra starch present in them. Parboiled rice is also available, which is prepared by soaking paddy in water, steaming thc paddy and then drying it. This rice retains most of the B vitamins and does not turn glutinous while cooking.

We also have the brown, black and red varieties of rice (only the hull is removed in such rice). The colour of the rice makes it rich in carotenoids and anthocyanins, and thus more nutritious. These varieties take longer to cook but are healthier as they contain more dietary fibre, Vitamin E and B complex.

Once upon a time, refined grains defined the social status of an individual. Hippocrates – the father of modern medicine – advised his wealthy patrons to follow the practice of their servants and favour whole grains to prevent many diseases. In the early days, wheat was ground between big stoned wheels, thus removing the bran but leaving the germ intact. The germ released oils when crushed, causing rancidity. Soon came the roller milling technique that removed the bran as well as the germ, thus improving the shelf life of the grains but reducing the nutritional worth.

Not Rice, but Still Nice

Did you know that *samak* rice (barnyard millet), popular on fasting menus, is actually a seed and not a grain? This type of rice is eaten with the hull and is thus quite nutritious. It is akin to the western quinoa. It is high on calcium, potassium, phosphorous and many amino acids (except lysine). *Samak* rice is used to prepare *kheer*, *khichri* and *upma*. It can be also be powdered and used as a coating for cutlets.

FAQs ABOUT RICE

Is rice fattening?

No, rice is not fattening. In fact, it has a low fat content (0.4g/100g rice). However, the glycaemic load (the ability of the foodstuff to raise blood sugar levels) of refined rice is high. Therefore, choosing the right variety of rice and portion control is important.

Can rice consumption lead to diabetes?

Polished white rice does raise blood sugar levels and the body's demand for insulin. It is thus advisable to limit the consumption of refined carbs such as white rice in the diet and go for the brown/red variety.

Like *samak*, sago is also not a grain, but a bunch of small balls of starch prepared from the trunk of various palm trees. It is similar to tapioca except that the balls of sago are smaller in size. It can be used as a carbohydrate source/snack in combination with nuts and veggies for children. In many regions, tapioca balls are commonly added to many drinks and shakes.

Gluten-Free: Fad or Fact?

I once met two strapping young boys who told me that the secret of their muscular well-built body was a gluten-free diet (GFD). They ascribed to this diet their increase in stamina and energy, weight loss and general well-being.

It is quite evident that the GFD is becoming more of a lifestyle choice rather than the treatment for a diagnosed condition known as Celiac Disease, due to which the person is unable to digest gluten. Celebrities such as Victoria Beckham and Gwyneth Paltrow have made the choice to be on a GFD and its popularity is growing. Buckwheat pizza and quinoa biryani are no longer 'exotic dishes' for such celebrities who have made the gluten-free commitment.

Myths about gluten (a protein found in wheat, barley and rye) abound. For one, it is assumed that a GFD is a grain-free diet. This is not at all true. A gluten-free diet includes grains such as buckwheat, corn, rice, jowar, ragi and bajra. Another myth doing the rounds is that gluten is responsible for lethargy, poor immunity and weight gain. The fact is that gluten is harmful only to those sensitive to this protein.

It is true that the tennis star Novak Djokovic's game transformed after he gave up gluten. This is because he was diagnosed with gluten sensitivity and this was not simply a fad diet for him.

Those diagnosed with Celiac Disease require strict adherence to a GFD for life. The beneficial effects that others notice when following the GFD is the result of the substitution of breads and bakery products with healthier foods such as a variety of millets, brown rice, amaranth and the like.

Quite clearly, when it is the prescribed dietary treatment, a GFD should be followed with utmost care. Children not diagnosed with Celiac Disease or Gluten Sensitivity should not be put on a GFD with the misconception that it is healthy. For kids who are sensitive to gluten, it is advisable to consult a nutritionist to arrive at a suitable diet.

LEGUME FAMILY, BEAN DU JOUR

Indian diets are unique because of the lentil content: we use a great deal of lentils and beans in our diet. I could enlist 101 ways in which one could eat lentils – either as a stand-alone dish or in combination with meat or grains!

> **A friend of mine includes lentils as gram flour to add fibre to omelettes for her teenager.' To ½ cup *besan* and ½ cup *suji*, add one beaten egg. Add chopped onions and leave covered for 10 minutes. Heat a skillet with oil and spread a thin layer of the batter and cook like one cooks a *cheela*.**

It is well established that healthy children need 10 per cent of their energy intake from proteins. In practical terms, it means that a quarter of the food plate should consist of protein-rich foods such as lentils, peas, egg and cheese.

It is generally believed that vegetarians are unable to meet their protein requirements as it is the animal foods that have higher protein value. But the protein needs of vegetarians can be satisfactorily met by consuming a combination of cereals and pulses, which complement each other within the same meal, e.g., rice/roti along with dal, hummus and bread, peanut butter with bread, corn with peas, tofu with rice, idli with sambar, and so on. This combination of a pulse/bean with a cereal is a smart combination, not just to make a tasty meal but also for enhancing nutritional value. Pulses are deficient in one amino acid (methionine) but rich in another one (lysine). Cereals, on the other hand, have the reverse nutritional profile (high on methionine and low on lysine). Thus, the combination of cereal and pulse makes perfect sense in every way.

For our country's large vegetarian population, pulses form the major source of protein in the diet. The nutritive contribution of dals in our diets is not just in terms of protein but also in terms of energy, Vitamins B_1 and B_2, folic acid and fibre. For vegetarians, pulses are an important source of iron as well. Pulses have a reasonable content of fat, which contributes to fulfilling the requirements of essential fatty acids (EFA). EFAs help regulate a wide variety of body functions including blood pressure, clotting of blood, immunity and blood lipid concentration.

I come to the next obvious question that you are likely to ask: What amount of lentils should a child eat in a day?

The quantity of lentils to be included in the diet would depend upon the age group and thus on the protein requirement. Protein requirements vary widely with age.

For instance, the protein requirement of a 7–10 year old is approximately 28g per day whereas in the 11-to-14-year age group, the protein requirement shoots up to 42g per day.

The Value of Lentils (Pulses), Dals and Beans

The table below comparing the protein content of different foods will help you appreciate the nutritional contribution of lentils to your child's diet.

You get 7g of protein from
30g pulses/*rajma*/*chana*
15g soya
35g peas
25g processed cheese
40g cottage cheese (paneer)
1 egg

In Indian vegetarian diets, pulses are indispensable for fulfilling nutritional needs. They are commonly eaten as an accompaniment with a cereal. Sprouting and fermentation are two ways of further increasing the nutritive worth of this category of food. The process of germination enhances the B-complex vitamins and adds to the Vitamin C content of the pulses. Sprouts of legumes can be used for fillings in momos, sandwiches, parathas, pulaos, *tikkis* and *kachoris*. The growth of children on adequate cereal–pulse combination diets is comparable to the growth of those on animal protein diets. When eaten together, cereals and pulses complement each other to provide a complete protein profile. The ideal ratio of this cereal–pulse combination is 8:1 (eight parts cereal with one part pulse), which is on the same lines as our dosa and idli mixtures!

Protein deficiency is present today not just in the obviously malnourished children but also in the apparently healthy-looking ones. Protein deficit can impair brain functioning, which in turn could lead to learning issues. Quite obviously, this deficiency can also affect growth rates in children. However, going overboard with this nutrient is also not advisable.

Pushing in more than what is needed in terms of proteins is not a good idea as it puts a burden on the kidneys. A one-year-old child, weighing approximately 10kg, ideally requires 1.5g protein/kg body weight, i.e., 15g protein per day.

The protein requirements of children (between 1 to 19 years) range between 1.1 to 1.5g per kg body weight.

I do not know of any culture in the world where pulses – and such a variety of them – form such an integral part of the diet as they do in our country. Not only are pulses extremely healthy, but they are also used to make very varied food items. In addition to many kinds of soups and great snack items, pulses are used to make popular desserts (such as dal *halwa* or *besan burfi*).

Different parts of India have their own favourites among pulses. The colour of the dal helps in its identification and nomenclature. Another interesting fact about legumes is that are consumed in a variety of forms: the whole pulse, split pulse, or after removal of the outer covering, i.e., *dhuli* dals.

These days, it is becoming difficult to fulfil the body's requirement of fibre, which is why one should opt for the whole *(sabut/chhilka)* dals whenever possible. Black gram pulse is black in colour in the whole form and when the covering is removed it becomes the white *urad* dal. The Bengal gram – whole – is the *chana* whereas Bengal gram dal is the *chane ki dal* that we are all familiar with. Yet other forms of the Bengal gram are the roasted form or *bhuna chana*, and *besan*.

Dried peas or *matar* is another pulse that lends itself well to Indian cuisine. Field beans or *sem* is yet another nutritious food. The traditional style of cooking these pulses is still popular in most Indian homes and shows amazing variations from region to region. Red gram or *arhar* dal, a favourite in many homes, lacks the beneficial fibre that is present in the whole versions. That is why a crucial tenet of healthy eating is to include a wide variety of dals in the diet.

The Secrets of Soya

Soya has been classified as a legume as well as an oilseed, and has been touted as the 'wonder bean'. Many products such as miso (soya paste), tofu/bean curd and soya drinks are made from it.

Soya has a higher protein content (40 per cent) compared with that of other lentils/dals, which contain an average of 20–25 per cent protein. Compared to other lentils, soya has less carbohydrate and a more fat content (18 per cent vs 1.5 per cent). The other benefit of soya is attributed to the fact that it contains omega-3 fats. Moreover, its high fibre content is useful in lowering cholesterol levels. The phytoestrogens present in it have antioxidant value. Soya is a healthy food to in corporate in our kids' diet but is in no way a miracle food.

Tempeh is a fermented soya product. Soya sauce is also prepared from soya by fermentation and addition of wheat (it is not gluten-free as most people believe it to be).

Tofu is made by coagulating soya milk and then pressing the curd to remove the excess liquid. Calcium salts may be added to soya while making tofu, which is why many varieties of tofu are high on calcium. Soya milk that has not been fortified remains a poor source of calcium (40mg calcium per cup vs 250mg per cup in dairy).

Confusion prevails around soya because of the many variants of soya available today. In the natural form, it is available as the miniature beans (pods) called edamame, which are similar to peas. The other processed forms of soya – soya protein concentrates and isolates – sold as supplements in health-food stores have not proved to be as beneficial as the natural product. Soya is best consumed as part of a healthy diet in the natural form and not as supplements.

Textured vegetable protein in forms other than soya nuggets/granules are quite popular in the west and have made an appearance in the Indian market as well. They are being made from soya to produce meat-like fibres, both in terms of texture and taste.

ALERT! Soya milk is looked upon as a health drink, but it is important to know the flip side of this product before one embarks on a soya milk diet. An acquaintance who wanted to turn vegan switched to soya milk completely. At the end of two years, I heard that she had begun to suffer from extreme pain in the bones, so much so that she would scream with pain during bumpy car rides. The doctors found that she had extreme calcium and B_{12} deficiency. In her desire to be vegan, she had not paid attention to the fact that unlike in foreign countries where there is a range of products available specifically for vegans – all fortified with calcium and Vitamin B_{12} – her diet here had deprived her of essential nutrients. Moreover, the calcium from soya milk is not absorbed as efficiently as the calcium from dairy.

A few facts to remember about pulses and legumes:

- They are best eaten in combination with cereals.
- Pulses with the outer husk intact, i.e., the *chhilka/sabut* dals, provide beneficial fibre and thiamine in higher amounts than the *dhuli* dals. The downside of fibre is that some people are affected by flatulence and gas that whole pulses can cause. Adding certain herbs and spices (asafoetida, cumin and *ajwain*), and adequate cooking and sprouting reduces this problem.
- Most lentils are good sources of iron, B vitamins and calcium. Although pulses do not contain Vitamin C, one can reap this nutrient by sprouting the seeds. Prolonged cooking of sprouts destroys the Vitamin C, so avoid doing that.
- Pulses can be eaten in any of the three forms: the whole form, split in half with skin intact, or devoid of skin (washed/*dhuli* dal). The whole and the split forms are superior in terms of nutritional worth. You may notice that the term 'gram' usually refers to legumes with husk/*chhilka*, whereas dal refers to the split variety without the husk.

MEAT: HOW IMPORTANT IS IT?

Very often you must have heard that animal protein is considered better-quality protein as compared to plant protein. What does this really indicate? Simply put, animal proteins are digested and absorbed by the body more efficiently due to their amino acid profile.

Many people prefer to be vegetarians for the sake of being healthy. However, it is possible for a purely vegetarian diet to be more unhealthy than a diet that contains some amount of meat. I have noticed that quite often pure vegetarians have meals that are loaded with full-fat *paneer*, fried foods and substantial amounts of refined flours. On the other hand, there are many non-vegetarians who are conscious of the amount of healthy foods they consume, and they include a small portion of low-fat meat along with lots of coloured veggies and fruits. Such a diet will always be regarded as the healthier one as opposed to the pure vegetarian one described above. After all, it is all about the ingredients that go into the diet and in what portions!

In a study conducted by the Medical University of Graz, Austria, in 2014, it was observed that the meat eaters were healthier than their vegetarian counterparts. When children eat small servings of meat/poultry/fish, they receive ample protein, iron, zinc and Vitamin B_{12}, which are all vital for growth. However, there are ways to ensure that a vegetarian diet is healthy and adequate. The vegetarian alternatives to meat are soya, beans, eggs, milk, cheese, yogurt, mushrooms, nuts and seeds.

Staying within Limits

When making decisions about your child's diet, remember that meats vary in their fat content, ranging from the very lean to the high-fat meats. Be wary of the hidden saturated fat in meats and limit intake to the recommended amounts.

For instance, a hamburger served at a typical fast-food outlet would contain as much fat as protein. Chicken wings – a favourite snack item – is very high on fat. Most of the fat of the chicken is stored under the skin. Usually, the wings are fried and eaten with a buttery dip. This makes a meal of chicken wings all about the fat.

Ground-meat products also contain the skin, which adds to the moistness. It is advisable to choose white meat without the skin. Fish, broiler chicken and shellfish are good choices.

Protein from animal sources (milk/meat/eggs) is best in terms of digestibility and utilization by the body. Soya protein comes a close second to it.

Meat eating is sometimes looked down upon as a hedonistic trait. However, my view on this subject is a little different. That we have to eat to live is a given. We have not yet discovered a way to sustain our life without taking away another form of life, be it plants or animals. Both forms of life are valuable. Therefore, I believe that, either way, one should not eat beyond one's requirements. Eating amounts that are considered appropriate is a way of showing respect to the other forms of life that sustain us. This is one of the reasons why I discourage overeating. It is the amount and not the food that is harmful. There are some techniques that help us to eat mindfully and they are discussed later in the book.

The healthy way to eat meat is to base the diet on plenty of vegetables, fruits, legumes and milk products. Add a small serving of fish/meat or poultry to this diet, if you wish to. Those meat eaters who eat mostly meat and reject fruits, vegetables and legumes are the ones who are at risk of developing health problems.

MEATY FACTS

Some things about meats that you may like to know.

- **Meats are a source of good-quality protein and CLA.**
- **They are also a fine source of iron. This form of Iron is absorbed well by the body.**
- **Meats are a good source of zinc, which keeps the immune system strong.**
- **They are an important source of Vitamin B_{12}, essential for neurological functions.**
- **There is a difference in the fat profile of red meats, too. The goat meat that we eat in India is lower in saturated fat content than some other red meats like beef and pork.**
- **Among the red meats, lamb (animals $<$14 months of age) has the best nutritive value.**
- **It is best to avoid processed meats such as sausages, bacon and salami. They have higher fat content, added salt, and other preservatives like nitrates.**
- **Avoid dry cooking methods, which are barbequing/charcoal grilling, and frying, especially on a regular basis.**
- **Marinating meats with turmeric and herbs prevents the formation of harmful compounds.**
- **Red meat should be trimmed of all visible fat before cooking.**
- **It is best to limit portions to not more than 250–500g per week for children.**

Adequacy, balance and variety are the three tenets of good nutrition, whether you are a vegetarian or a non-vegetarian.

NUTS IN A NUTSHELL

What do you do when your child feels ravenous just as you have settled down in the car ready to enjoy the 'road trip'? You probably hand over a packet of biscuits. The next time, try a handful of nuts (spiced or roasted) instead and watch how your child will be satiated until the next halt! The fibre, protein and fat in nuts suppress hunger pangs, making a much better snack option than the high-calorie ones like chips and cookies.

The idea of eating less fat became the norm in the late 1990s and early 2000s. Low-fat cookies with less fat but more sugar hit the market and remained popular for a good 10 years. With this came the revelation that when people eat less fat, they are hungry for something else and overdo the carbohydrate bit, leading to a new set of issues. This is why you and your child would be better off eating nuts rather than cookies!

Did you know that 40 kernels of pistachios or 20 kernels of almonds are equivalent to just 15 potato chips in terms of fat content? However, the kind of fat found in nuts is different and better. Please note that pistachio has three times more fibre and protein than an equivalent amount of potato chips.

It is true that 80 per cent of the calories in nuts come from fat, but nuts consumed in measured quantities do not cause weight gain. This is because the body treats the good fats derived from nuts differently.

Nuts are not high on cholesterol as is often believed. They sure are high on calories, which come from the good fats and proteins. Nuts – in moderation – should be an integral part of a healthy diet. Try to include $^{1}/_{2}$ to 1 serve of different nuts in your child's diet.

One standard serve of nuts/seeds is 30g.

Name of nut	Nut count for 1 serve (30g)
Walnut half (shelled)	14
Almonds (shelled)	23
Pistachio (unshelled)	45
Cashew	16
Peanuts	28
Seeds	3 tbsp

Do not soak and peel almonds like granny did! Eat them whole. The peel is loaded not just with fibre but also with immunity-enhancing compounds!

GO FOR NUTS!

- **Nuts reduce the risk of certain cancers, heart and neuro-degenerative diseases.**
- **They can help lose weight (by promoting satiety).**
- **They contain E vitamins, antioxidants and unsaturated fats.**

THE VALUE OF SEEDS

Like nuts, seeds are a beneficial source of fat in our diet. Regular consumption of seeds can lower inflammation markers in the body. When these markers in the body are elevated, the risk of heart disease and diabetes also rises. Seeds are cholesterol-free and are a good source of plant protein (20–30 per cent).

Add them to smoothies, bread, yogurt, cookies, salads, soups or cereals. You can roast them lightly or heat them in a *karahi* or skillet without oil, and snack on them.

Tiny but Potent

Why do you think grannies took the pain of removing seeds from melons and pumpkins, drying them and serving them? Seeds are the nutritional equivalents of nuts at a lower price tag! Great sources of protein and the healthy variety of fats, Vitamin E and dietary fibre, seeds enhance immunity, relieve constipation and much more.

• **Flaxseeds:** Much before flaxseeds acquired the label of being a health food, I was introduced to them in my childhood, when every time I visited my grandmother, a speck of black powder was an essential component of the lunch *thali*. I later discovered that it was roasted and ground flaxseed powder.

The seeds are rich in dietary fibre, particularly lignan plant estrogens as well as antioxidants. The lignan content of flaxseeds is 800 times more than that of any other plant food. They are also a very good source of alpha-linolenic acid (omega-3 fatty acid).

Just 100g of the ground seeds provides 28g dietary fibre and 20g protein! It is important to crush or grind flaxseeds before consumption. You can add the crushed seeds to porridges, smoothies or the flour for making rotis, cakes, waffles and so on. Try to incorporate 1–2 tbsp of crushed flaxseeds in any of the above ways daily.

Take note that once ground, the seeds oxidize easily and turn rancid, thus losing some nutrition, too. Therefore, it is best to grind small quantities at a time and store in an airtight container rather than storing large amounts of ground seeds.

• **Pumpkin seeds:** Before I became familiar with the science of healthy eating, I remember my aunt from West Bengal collecting pumpkin seeds whenever she cooked the vegetable, roasting them on a *tawa*, adding either red chilli powder or black pepper and lemon, and happily snacking on them. The creamy white, husky seeds by themselves are unlikely to be enjoyed by children. However, the seeds could be added to other snacks such as puffed rice, flattened rice (*chiwda*) or to salads, muffins and cakes. This seed is rich in the antioxidant panagamic acid, which is unique to it. Shelled pumpkin seeds are equivalent to pine nuts in terms of nutritive value at a tenth of the cost.

• **Chia seeds:** The word 'Chia' means fatty or oily. These gluten-free seeds are native to Mexico. One serving of chia seeds contains nutrients quite similar to flaxseeds. Whole chia seeds or their sprouts are usually added to drinks, salads and puddings to make them nutritious. When it comes to adding them to children's food, chia seeds score over flaxseeds because chia seeds are tasteless and can be added to all kinds of dishes. Also, there is no need to grind chia seeds before use as is required in the case of flaxseeds.

Sunflower seeds: These seeds are perhaps the most commonly used among all. Also, being rich in fat, they are satisfying yet healthy. Sunflower seeds are a good source of magnesium. They have a high fat content, so store them in a cool place or in the refrigerator. These seeds can be added to salads, sprinkled on cereals, or added to scrambled eggs, cereal, muffins and homemade *namkeens*.

Sesame seeds: All three variants – black, white and the uncommon red – are good sources of calcium, magnesium and copper. Sesame seeds are used to make tahini, which is added to hummus and moutabel (Middle Eastern dips). In Indian food, you could add sesame seeds to sautéed vegetables, chicken and *dhokla*. Many vegetables such as beans and potatoes go well with roasted sesame seeds. Some Indian sweets also use sesame seeds.

- **Watermelon seeds:** I regret that my generation of people grew up eating watermelon only when the seeds were removed. This happened in spite of the fact that the Ayurvedic tradition recognized the value of this food and recommended including it in many ways. Fortunately, wisdom has prevailed and science has backed the claim that watermelon seeds are valuable to a healthy diet. Watermelon seeds are a rich source of arginine (an amino acid that is a building block for protein) that can help lower BP and maintain heart health. The unsaturated fats present in them make them good for the heart, and they make for a useful snack in weight-loss diets. About 30g of these seeds provides 8g protein. I usually add watermelon pieces to the salad without removing the seeds – the easiest way to get the kids to eat the seeds when the fruit is in season. Off season, the roasted seeds taste good when added to salads and yogurt.
- **Sweet basil seeds or *sabja*:** These can be added to milkshakes, desserts and smoothies after soaking them in

water. These seeds are high on Vitamin K and iron, among other nutrients. They can be used instead of chia seeds in many recipes.

- **Alfa Alfa seeds:** These seeds are usually unlikely to be part of a child's diet, as they are an 'adult taste' product. These seeds should be sprouted before consumption. Commonly referred to as *rajko*, these seeds help in lowering cholesterol and blood sugar levels. They also have anti-cancer and anti-fungal properties.

- **Hemp seeds:** These seeds are making a comeback as the latest superfood due to their outstandingly high protein content (second only to soya) and that, too, of very good quality. All the essential protein building blocks (amino acids) are present in hemp seeds. Good amounts of arginine render this seed an excellent heart protective food. A great source of fibre and Vitamin E, their good fat makes them an effective anti-inflammatory food. Being low on sodium and cholesterol-free, this seed makes a value addition in the diet. It is sensitive to heat, therefore it should be only lightly roasted and sprinkled on salads and smoothies. You can also add it to cookies, cake and desserts as it has a nutty, creamy flavour. This seed is not to be confused with marijuana although both belong to the same family. Substitute pine nuts with these seeds the next time you make pesto sauce.

Without doubt, seeds should be an integral part of the diets of both children and adults. They are the most cost effective way of reaping the benefit of many nutrients in small amounts. Combine different seeds together (in *namkeens/mixtures*) or use one kind at a time (in desserts and smoothies).

FATS AND OILS: CONSTANTLY CHANGING SCENE

Recently, I met my school friends after nearly 30 years. As we chatted about our carefree lives back in the day, the talk veered around to the food that we carried in our tiffins – the *gobhi* parathas, *gajar ka halwa* and the thick layers of butter in the sandwiches. Quite evidently, we were not on any fat-restricted diets by any stretch of the imagination as our favourite mouth-watering dishes were heavy on either *desi* ghee or butter. Yet none of us was fat or obese. Childhood obesity was not as prevalent then as it is now.

The reasons are quite obvious. In those days, we ate home-cooked meals on most days, adhering to the mealtimes set by our parents. There was no question of ordering in from a food joint or eating in front of the TV. Eating out was a treat and at home one always had to eat at the dining table. We also remembered how we played outdoors for hours at a stretch, cycled to school, and walked long distances.

This set me thinking: With increased consciousness about the bad effects of fat on our body, we are shunning ghee and butter, yet incidences of obesity and heart disease are rising. Where, then, does the problem lie? Is it also not true that some amount of fat in the diet is necessary for us?

It is well established that our body needs some quantity of fats. Growing children need fats in their daily diet not only as an energy source but also for the essential fatty acids present in them. These cannot be manufactured by the body and the body's requirement is fulfilled through fat consumption in the diet. We need fats for the cell membranes, many hormones, and fat soluble vitamins.

Some studies emanating from sources alien to our practices made *desi* ghee and butter villains in matters of heart health. On the scene then emerged new products – margarine and *vanaspati* (hydrogenated fats) – whose health benefits and ability to prevent heart disease were touted.

It became clear only after years that butter and ghee were actually better than artificially hydrogenated fats. Remember, the body finds it difficult to process hydrogenated fats, which are produced by chemical processes. The real advantages of hydrogenation are purely commercial and they translate into profits for manufacturers. For one, hydrogenation endows fats with the ability to stay fresh for a much longer period (all fats, unless treated, turn rancid with time). In addition, fats can better withstand repeated heating when hydrogenated. This is a boon for the *mithaiwala* who can profitably fry several batches of samosas and *jalebis* in the same oil. Hydrogenated oil is actually cheaper than the non-hydrogenated variants, mostly because there are no regulations to check its quality. Trans fats from such hydrogenated fats are extremely harmful and the use of *vanaspati* ghee (hydrogenated vegetable oil) has contributed in a major way to the high incidence of heart disease in the country.

Following this era, the pendulum swung in favour of the highly unsaturated fats like sunflower oils, corn and safflower, only to realize that the predominance of the n-6 fatty acids in these oils was not desirable!

There are three broad categories of fatty acids in foods: SFA (saturated fatty acids), MUFA (monounsaturated fatty acids) and PUFA (polyunsaturated fatty acids) (n-3 and n-6) that the body requires. There has been a great deal of debate regarding the ideal fat requirement in humans.

Current wisdom emphasizes the need to replace the 'bad fats' with the good ones. In simple, practical terms, it means that we replace red meat with nuts and legumes, butter with soya oil, poultry with fish and so on. The good fats are in the form of MUFA and PUFA. Omega-3 fats are one kind of PUFA, which have beneficial effect on the body, particularly the heart. They have cholesterol-lowering, anti-inflammatory and anti-clotting properties.

Although a particular oil may have predominately one kind of fatty acid, it will also contain other fatty acids. For instance, peanut oil has the highest percentage of MUFA but also contains lesser amounts of PUFA and SFA.

Keeping in mind evidence from the past as well as the latest scientific knowledge, current wisdom dictates the following criteria for identifying a healthy cooking oil:

- The total fat intake for an individual should ideally be between 20–30 per cent of the total calories. The same is advised for children, too. Per person, the total consumption of fat/oil should ideally be approximately 500g/month, i.e., 3–4 tsp/day.
- The SFA content should be low, which means it should not exceed 8–10 per cent of the calories derived from fat sources.

For instance, a one-year-old child requires 1,000 calories in a day. 20–30 per cent of this (200–300 calories) should come from fat in one day.

From the total fat calories, only 10 per cent, i.e., (20–30 calories) should be from SFA, which is about ½ tsp (1 tsp fat = 5g = 45 calories).

The rest of the allowance should come from MUFA and PUFA (180–270 calories), which is = 1–2 tbsp.

- The ratio of omega-6 to omega-3 in the oil should be 5 or less. Some western diets have ratios as high as 30:1, which is not desirable. Such abnormal ratios could enhance the pro-inflammatory responses in the body. This happens when the main source of oil is predominantly n-6 PUFA-rich, as it is in sunflower, safflower, or corn.

SOME FAT FACTS

- **The commercially produced trans fats must be avoided, although some amount of naturally occurring trans fats present in meat and milk are acceptable.**
- **All oils provide 9 kcal per gram of oil. There is only a minor variation in the calorie count of butter/ghee.**
- **Oils do not contain carbohydrate and protein.**

It is not easy to single out one oil that meets all the above mentioned criteria. For instance, among all edible oils, olive oil has the highest content of MUFA but has no omega-3, whereas soya and mustard are high in omega-3, but do not have the ideal omega-6 to omega-3 ratios.

Taking all things into account, the oils that emerge as the better options are olive, mustard, peanut, sesame, rice bran and soya. *Desi* ghee or butter is no longer a 'no-no' provided it is consumed only in limited amounts and is not used as the only source of fat in the diet.

One of the many advantages of eating at home is that the benefits of the cooking oil can be maximized both in terms of quality and quantity.

- Blending any two or three of these recommended oils is an easy way to fulfil the body's varied requirement of fats.
- Yet another way of incorporating the benefits of different oils is to use, say, olive oil for breakfast, sesame oil for lunch and mustard oil for dinner. Blended oils are now available commercially as well. Alternately, olive/canola/sesame oil can be used for salads and sunflower/safflower/rice bran for cooking foods. This way, one gets the benefit from different oils in a day.

Flaxseed oil and fish oils are excellent sources of omega-3 fatty acids, but cannot be used for cooking as they cannot tolerate high temperatures. So including fatty fish in the diet is a good way of imbibing this fat. For vegetarians, lentils, soya, green leafy vegetables, broccoli, wheatgerm, walnuts, fenugreek and seeds are rich sources of good fats.

OLIVE OIL

Olive oil is perhaps the most fashionable of all the oils currently in use and is often singled out as a heart-friendly oil as it is high in MUFA.

THE POSITIVES

Yes, it is rich in MUFA, high in antioxidants (polyphenols), Vitamin A and Vitamin E. This translates into benefit for the heart, the prevention of certain cancers (breast), lowering bad cholesterol, reducing abdominal obesity and reducing blood pressure. It has anti-inflammatory properties, reduces the risk of gallstones and boosts immunity.

THE NEGATIVES

Olive oil does not have omega-3 fatty acids. This is why some amount of mustard/canola/sesame oil in the diet would complement it to provide the perfect profile.

THE VARIETIES

Olive oil is of different varieties: Extra virgin, virgin, pure (refined or light) and pomace. These have varying amounts of polyphenols (plant antioxidants), so the benefits also vary.

HOW TO STORE

Olive oil has three enemies: sunlight, heat and oxygen (air). Thus, just being able to get your hands on virgin cold-pressed oil is not enough. You must ensure that it is packaged in dark bottles and stored at temperatures below 30 °C. Remember to check the date of bottling and keep in mind that its shelf life is two years.

The Truth about Pomace Olive Oil

Pomace is the lowest edible grade of olive oil. Its extraction uses both high heat and solvents, which is not desirable. Do not get misled by its relatively low price. After all, pomace has none of the health benefits associated with extra virgin olive oil.

The USP of Different Oils

- **Canola/Mustard/Rapeseed:** Contain decent amounts of all the fractions of essential fatty acids. The reservation about rapeseed oil is its high erucic (fatty acid toxic in high amounts) content. Canola is the low erucic variant of rapeseed oil.
- **Coconut oil:** The only vegetable-origin fat with SFA for which it had earned a bad reputation. However, it has been proven that the SFA in coconut oil is beneficial. It has antioxidant, immune-enhancing and anti-infective properties.
- **Olive oil:** Has high MUFA. Should supplement it with n-3 PUFA rich oil (mustard/soya/canola) to get the right balance.
- **Peanut oil:** Good balance of SFA, MUFA and n-6 PUFA but no n-3 PUFA.
- **Rice bran:** Rich in MUFA and n-6 PUFA but does not contain n-3 PUFA. Its profile is like that of sunflower/corn oil blended with olive oil.
- **Safflower/Sunflower/Corn:** Too much of n-6 PUFA, very little monounsaturated and negligible n-3 PUFA. Not recommended as a single source of oil. Supplement or combine with MUFA and n-3 rich oil.
- **Sesame oil:** Reasonable MUFA and n-6 PUFA but limited in n-3 PUFA.
- **Soya:** Good mix of all the fractions of essential fatty acids. This is a good all-round oil.

The ideal fat for consumption for us humans is one that has SFA, MUFA, PUFA (both n-6 and n-3) in the desired ratio. Mustard, canola and soya are among the oils available in India that have all the three categories of fatty acids present in them. Some amount of supplementation with ghee/butter/coconut oil along with these oils can provide the perfect profile for consumption and regular use.

BE FAT-SAVVY!

Just as in the case of grains and sugar, I strongly believe that the time has come for us to stop seeking refined, deodorized oils that have been extracted and processed at high temperatures through the use of solvents. Such high temperatures facilitate the production of trans fats too.

In fact, one has come around to believe what many old-timers say, that the cold-pressed oils – olive, mustard or sesame – are extremely good because, unlike the refined oils, they retain their antioxidant properties. Cold pressing is the traditional method of extracting oil from seeds/fruits. The seeds are ground to a paste and then pressed with a heavy stone mill to extract the oil. Earlier generations managed to escape the ill effects of commercially refined oils. The younger generation is now being reminded of the virtues of cold-pressed oil with the olive oil lobby blowing its trumpet about it. In South India, cold-pressed sesame oil (*chekku ennai*) was a way of life until 50 years ago, after which the trend of using refined oils took over. Cold-pressed oils are good because they help retain the natural properties of oilseeds.

When choosing oils, look out for information on the PUFA content on the label, specified in terms of n-6 and n-3 fatty acids. It is important to know if the oil contains n-3

PUFA in adequate amount as most oils predominately have n-6 PUFA. The desirable ratio of n-6 to n-3 in the oil/diet should ideally range between 10:1 to 5:1.

This means that, if the total PUFA is 34, an n-6 value of 29 and n-3 value of 5 would be considered ideal.

SUGAR AND ITS ROLE IN OUR DIET

Let's face it. Most of us crave the sweet flavour every so often and it is because we are hardwired that way. When we eat such foods (sugars, which is a carbohydrate), the feel-good brain chemical, serotonin, is released. It is perfectly fine to indulge your sweet tooth by including desserts in your meal plan, provided you do not exceed the upper limit of the prescribed allowance. The World Health Organization (WHO) has very recently recommended that people should not consume more than 5 per cent of the total daily calories from sugar. For a normal-weight adult, this recommendation translates into 6 tsp or 25g sugar per day. For children, depending on the age group and on the calorie requirement, the amount of sugar may vary between 15–20g per day. Stated simply, in a 1,000 calorie diet, 13.5g sugar is permissible (1 tsp of sugar = 5g = 20 calories).

The fact is that it is the sugar in the food that is responsible for making it so irresistible. Of late, there has been some debate on the point whether it is the fat and creamy textures that prompt people to eat compulsively or the sugar. At the Oregon Research Institute, Eugene, Oregon, USA, researchers served milkshakes to high-school students while an MRI was performed to watch the reward centres in their brain. Their work, published in the *American Journal of Clinical Nutrition* in 2013, clearly states that the sugar in foods lights up the pleasure centres in the brain more than fat does. Therefore, one needs to be careful about how much sugar we allow children to consume so that they can enjoy a treat but, at the same time, not get addicted to it. The difficult part is that almost all processed foods contain sugar and syrups in plenty to make them tastier. The insidious ways in which sugar is added to even the so-called healthy breakfast cereals is reason enough for you to be alert.

Sugars in Processed Foods: Trick or Treat?

It is quite likely that you may not recognize sugar on a label due to its diverse forms and nomenclature. Take the instance of a granola bar, which may contain sugar in many different forms such as high maltose corn syrup, tapioca syrup, fructose, honey and maltodextrin.

That is why I decided to decode some sugar names for you.

1 **Sugar alcohols** are being used in many so-called healthy products as they provide fewer calories than regular sugar, i.e., sucrose, but they are certainly not calorie-free. The names of the sugar alcohols usually end with 'itol'. Mannitol, sorbitol, xylitol, maltitol, lactitol and isomalt are some of the sugar alcohols commonly added to processed foods. They do not contain alcohol or any intoxicant but have a chemical

structure similar to alcohol. Any food that has more than 50g sugar alcohol can induce a laxative effect.

Some other terms used for sugars:

- Glucose (also known as dextrose), fructose and galactose are simple sugars (monosaccharides).
- Lactose, maltose, sucrose (white sugar) have two or more units of sugar (disaccharides).

2 **Honey** has a combination of glucose and fructose, derived from the sucrose (nectar) that bees collect.

3 **Molasses** is touted as a natural sugar, as it is the syrup left after the refining of sugar from sugarcane. It is a less sweet and less processed form of sugar. It is dark in colour as it contains fair amounts of iron, which is absorbed from the machinery in which it is produced.

4 **Corn syrup:** It is produced by the action of enzymes on cornstarch. It contains a mixture of glucose and maltose. It is another processed form of sugar and is best avoided.

5 **High Fructose Corn Syrup (HFCS):** This has been a favourite with the food industry. As the name suggests, it contains fructose in addition to glucose and maltose. It should be avoided as its very sweet taste gets children addicted to it, and it could also lead to a fatty liver and a host of related problems.

6 **Brown rice syrup:** This is currently being used as an alternative to HFCS. Although the name suggests that it is a healthy alternative, it is actually a highly processed form of sugar produced by enzymatic action on brown rice.

7 **Sorghum sugar:** This is processed in a manner similar to brown rice sugar.

8 **Fruit juice sweetener:** Dehydrated fruit juice is used to produce concentrated sugar syrup and is used in products that claim to be 'all-fruit'. It does add to the sugar content of the product and increases calorie values.

Until now it was believed that sugar was less harmful than salt for raising blood pressure. Recent studies actually suggest the reverse. Therefore, it is imperative to watch sugar intake for this reason, too.

The role of sugar in worsening depression and anxiety-like behaviours is also being noted in new studies.

As the harmful effects of too much sugar are becoming more and more evident, the popularity of artificial sweeteners is increasing. However, artificial sweeteners are not the panacea for sugar-related problems.

ARTIFICIAL SWEETENERS FOR CHILDREN

The long-term effects of artificially-sweetened beverages on children are unknown, so it is best for kids to avoid them.

- **Artificial sweeteners can disrupt the body's natural ability to regulate blood sugar, probably by altering the microbes in our gut.**
- **One concern about artificial sweeteners is that they affect the body's ability to gauge how many calories are being consumed. Some studies show that sugar and artificial sweeteners affect the brain in different ways. This could leave one dissatisfied and craving for more sugar!**
- **At the University of California-San Diego, US, researchers performed functional MRI scans as volunteers took small sips of water sweetened with sugar or sucralose. Sugar activated regions of the brain involved**

in food reward, while artificial sweeteners did not. It seems that while sugar signals a positive feeling of reward, artificial sweeteners may not be an effective way to manage a craving for sweets.

Take home message: Jaggery, honey and table sugar in moderation are better than artificial sweeteners.

Last but not the least, make the kids brush their teeth after sweet dinners!

A DASH OF SALT

Salt is one of the most common and significant ingredients of our diet and is more or less taken for granted by most of us. Not many of us realize its role and importance from the point of view of nutrition.

The role of salt is not just confined to that of a taste enhancer. Some extremely important functions in the body, such as the acid–base balance, nerve conduction, muscle contraction, blood volume maintenance and water balance, are closely related to salt intake.

In this era of over-consumption, even the sodium content of our diets tends to be greatly in excess of our requirements, with far-reaching consequences for our health. An optimal sodium intake is crucial for the well being of our body, but excessive consumption can be harmful. When processed foods were absent from Indian diets, the vegetarian diets were not high on salt. In recent times, largely due to the dominance of processed foods and the popular eating-out culture, our salt consumption has increased greatly.

Dangers of Excessive Salt Intake

Too much salt in the diet increases the risk of developing high blood pressure (hypertension) and related cardiovascular conditions. High blood pressure, if left uncontrolled, may lead to disability, stroke, kidney failure and/or eye problems. Excessive salt intake could also lead to troubled sleep.

- **The harm that excess salt intake can do has been equated to tobacco intake in a study by Tufts University, US.**
- **One in four Indian adults suffers from high blood pressure.**
- **An ICMR Study showed that salt intake in urban India is 7.5g, which is much higher than we require.**

How much sodium do we really need in our daily diet to lead a healthy life and much are we actually consuming? In a tropical hot country like ours, the sodium that is required in order to carry on body functions efficiently and at the same time compensate for losses in sweat and urine is only 500mg per day. A major part of the sodium requirement can easily be met when consuming a mixed diet – green leafy vegetables, meats, dairy foods and nuts. Almost three-quarters of our body's need for sodium can be met through natural foods and it is unlikely that one could become sodium deficient if table salt is not added to food.

It is not advisable to overshoot the safe allowance, which sets the *upper* limit at 1,500mg sodium per day for healthy young adults – equal to 3.75g of sodium chloride or ½–¾ tsp of salt in a day. The adult limit is 2,000mg sodium, which is equivalent to 5g or 1 tsp salt. Contrast this recommended allowance with what we may actually be eating. Many flavourings such as soya sauce and MSG (monosodium glutamate), if used regularly, can push the consumption to a hundred times of what is required! Watch out for excessively salted foods, i.e., those containing higher than 1.5g salt per 100g of product (0.6g sodium/100g).

Some restaurant meals are known to contain as high as 5,300mg sodium. Ingredients such as baking soda, MSG, sodium nitrate and other additives have high sodium content. The other major source of sodium is processed foods that are loaded with preservatives, flavour enhancers and texture enhancers. Salt is actually added to low-fat foods to compensate for the lack of taste. You may be surprised to know that 25g of cornflakes contains more sodium than 25g of salted peanuts! The sodium in the processed foods is not always present in conjunction with chloride, as is the case with salt, lending it that 'salty' flavour. This is why we don't even realize how much sodium we are actually consuming.

This is also why many processed foods that are high in sodium need not necessarily taste salty; in fact, sweet-tasting foods such as instant puddings could be high-sodium too. On the label, look out for all sodium salts that have been added to the food. Low-sodium foods are those which contain <140mg sodium per serving. It is good to keep a check on this aspect of packaged foods, especially if they are part of the regular diet.

What is MSG? It is the sodium salt of the amino acid (glutamic acid) extracted from a Japanese seaweed. It is a flavour enhancer and is added to foods for this specific quality. This salt should not be added to foods of infants less than 12 months of age. The Prevention of Food Adulteration (PFA) Act says that MSG may be added to food as long as the glutamate content is not more than one per cent. More than this amount can cause problems.

Having discussed all the food families, it is evident that the importance of children's diets lies in preventing deficiencies and malnutrition, as well as in stemming the development of inherited disorders such as type 2 diabetes. Wholesome eating is all about including the various food groups in the diet. It is also as much about the amount (dose) that the body needs of these foods on a regular basis in order to function at optimum levels. This is why the next logical step is to understand portion size.

[3]

The Truth about Portion Size

No matter how healthy the diet is, eating too much or too little of any food can pose a problem. We currently live in the times of plenty and this is reflected in the larger portions that we consume. With growing portion sizes, it has become easy to misjudge quantities and overeat. Overeating due to inaccurate portion sizes is the most common pitfall of diets today, leading to obesity and related problems. There is much concern regarding this aspect in nutrition circles.

In order to get some idea about portion sizes of food, it is best to weigh the items, but it's not possible to do this all the time. The more practical approach is to deal with the concept of portion sizes by observing and comparing the portions to common articles such as a golf ball or a deck of cards for a rough estimate. This technique is called 'eyeballing' portion sizes.

Understanding Portion Size

Many of my clients are surprised when I tell them that a slice of bread can be substituted with only three tablespoons of cooked rice in order to maintain the calorie and carbohydrate content of the meal.

One knows that a healthy diet should include at least five portions of fruits and vegetables in a day. What really is one portion can be confusing and misleading. Take a look at the instances below to get an idea:

- 1 cup cut fruit or 1 medium-sized fruit such as an apple (the size of a baseball or a woman's fist) makes one portion. If the size of the apple is larger than this, it would amount to another extra portion.
- ¼ cup (the size of a golf ball) of dried fruits such as raisins makes one portion of the fruit allowance.
- In the meat food group, 100g chicken/other meat (the size of a deck of playing cards) constitutes 1 portion.
- In the dairy group, 1 cup yogurt or 240g is (approximately the size of a baseball) makes 1 portion. Approximately 45g of hard cheese (the size of three large playing dice) makes 1 dairy portion.

If one digs into a packet/bag of food, portion control is impossible to adhere to. What one needs to do is to empty the contents on a plate, estimate the approximate portion size required, and keep the extra portions away.

Estimating Portions

The interesting thing about portions is that a portion means different things to different people. Why should it not? After all, a portion is the amount one *chooses* to eat and this could vary from person to person and from time to time depending on how hungry you are or how much you are conditioned to eating. A clear understanding of portions is crucial for anyone interested in eating right. Certain images that you can use as visual reference anywhere and anytime can help you avoid the problems of excesses as well as deficiencies.

Portions in terms of household measures are easy:

- 1 cupped hand makes ½ cup
- 2 cupped hands makes 1 cup
- Palm of hand/a deck of cards is the size of approximately 100g of meat
- 1 medium potato/fruit is the size of a light bulb

As a general rule, it is better to eat *smaller portions of a variety of foods* than to eat very large portions of food only from one family. This means that just because green tea or olive oil is healthy, it does not mean we neglect other foods groups. When one consumes large portions of food from one group (no matter how healthy) it is bound to displace foods from other essential food groups.

One exchange of cereal measures 30g. For instance, your nine-year-old daughter requires nine exchanges of cereal in a day. If you give her a jumbo-sized muffin, the child is unlikely to eat just one-third of it and stop. By eating the large muffin, the child consumes more than half the day's allowance of grains in one go. With the widespread availability of packaged foods, understanding how to exchange or compare one food with another in the same family becomes essential. I do hope that in the future realistic serving sizes get mentioned on labels, based on what people actually consume rather than those that suit marketing gimmicks. For instance, one interesting label mentioned one spoon of ice cream as one portion to fit the 'healthy' tag!

The Secrets of Substitution

Over the years, in my interaction with clients and patients, I have noticed that it is easy for people to grasp the need for including various food groups in the diet. However, the tricky part is understanding substitution within food groups. For instance, if one were to substitute an item in the cereal group, it would be crucial to know how much of pasta or rice should replace a roti/chapatti. I often hear parents lament that the popularity of pasta is causing children to shun chapattis and, in the process, gain weight.

I do not completely agree with such a simplistic conclusion. It is the huge portions of pasta that children eat that spell trouble. Children in the Mediterranean regions grow up on pasta, after all, and do not gain weight. This is because pasta is never the main dish of the meal there. It is the portion size of the pasta that is important and also what accompanies it. If pasta is the main course, your child is bound be hungry soon enough. In such a case, the likelihood of snacking on yet another unhealthy food is strong, too.

The Exchange Guide

As I said earlier in the book, even so-called healthy foods tend to become unhealthy if taken in unwarranted amounts.

This 'portion distortion' is the hidden cause of the many problems that we face today. Although most books tend to address large portions as a nutritional problem, I have observed that eating too little of certain foods is as much of an issue. The leading offenders in this 'eaten-too-little' category are fruits and vegetables. Shown below is an easy way to work out how one can exchange one food with another in appropriate amounts.

For cereals and starchy foods, it works this way:
1 slice bread = 1 chapatti = 1 cup dry readymade cereal = ½ cup cooked rice/pasta/cooked cereal/spaghetti/macaroni = 3 cups popcorn = ¼ bagel = 1 tortilla = 2–3 biscuits = ½ *bhatura* = ½ cup boiled corn = 1 idli (large) = 1 medium potato = ⅓ cup potato chips = 1 medium plain dosa

In the milk and dairy family, here is how substitution should happen:
1 cup milk = 1 cup yogurt/curd = 35g processed cheese = 45g cottage cheese = 2 cheese slices

For the fruit group:
1 cup fresh, frozen or canned fruit = 1 medium fruit or 1 melon wedge = ¼ cup dried fruit = ½ cup fruit juice = 1½ cup cup high-water-content fruit, e.g., watermelon

In the vegetable family:
½ cup cut/raw/cooked veggies = 1 cup leafy variety = ½ cup vegetable juice

For meat and lentils:
1 egg = 50g cooked meat/fish/poultry = ¼ cup paneer or tofu = ½ cup cooked dal/beans = ¼ cup dry uncooked lentils = 1–2 tbsp peanut butter = 15–30g nuts or seeds

Food guide for children (1–19 years) in terms of servings

Food Family	1–2 years	2+–5 years	5+–10 years	10+–19 years
Grains	2–3	3–5	5–11	12–16
Vegetables	1–2	1½–2	3	3
Fruits	1–2	1½–2	2–3	2–3
Meat/Legumes	½	¾–1	2	2–3
Milk	3	2–3	2	2
Fat/Oil	2–3	2–4	3–4	5–8
Sugar	–	–	2–3	3–4
Water	Water intake needs to be adequate for all age groups. For a guide to water intake, please see Chapter 11: *Beverages*			

The best way to predict the future is to create it. Here is your opportunity to build your child's future.

SECTION 3

GETTING READY

[4]

Shop Smart

Eating is an enjoyable experience for us. Eating healthy, though, is quite another matter. In fact, planning a nutritious meal can become very stressful for the person responsible for executing it for the family. After all, healthy eating does not simply pertain to what is finally on your plate. It begins with making the correct choices right from shopping to storing the foods, followed by choosing appropriate methods of cooking using the best possible procedures. The food you select and the way you store it affects everything about the final dish or meal you will serve your child: the look, the flavour, the texture, the aroma and, most importantly, the nutritional value.

Go Local, Go Seasonal, Go Traditional

Going for fresh seasonal products is the easiest and possibly the best way to shop right. There was a time when going to the market close by to shop for fresh fruits and vegetables was very much a part of the daily routine. Ensuring the freshness and quality of the produce firsthand was of utmost importance. This trend is changing. Many of us don't have the time to do this ourselves. Now we order groceries over the phone and the Internet. Sometimes we buy and store supplies over a long period of time because we wish to avoid repeated trips to the market. However, by saving time this way, are we in turn compromising on nutrients?

Ideally, the shopping process is one in which we should involve our children. It would be a good idea to urge them to come along to the market and make it an enjoyable experience for them. If this is not possible, we should at least get our children to see fresh produce in its natural state. Many children these days are totally ignorant of the appearance and texture of fresh vegetables. The idea is to engage them with the 'ground reality' of fresh fruits and vegetables, which increases their willingness to eat the same. This is something that I have personally noted with many children on various occasions. The market, especially in the winter season, is a treat – the colours, shapes and texture of the fruits and vegetables are fascinating. Moreover, children's participation in how to choose the best-quality produce will always come in handy in life.

This conviction of mine was reinforced when I happened to watch a group of five-year old kids on a farm for a school picnic – they were overjoyed to see tomatoes growing on the plants. Some of the kids looked absolutely bewildered, as they had imagined that tomatoes could be found only in grocery stores! My kids also enjoyed their trip to the local vegetable vendor who would offer them an occasional peapod to relish. Such experiences allow children to try out and develop a taste for a variety of produce and relish it too!

It may seem great that we have access to foods that are out of season and that, too, all year round. What we tend to forget is that by doing so we may be compromising on both taste and nutritional worth in the process.

In addition to the nutritional issues, there are many problems with eating foods that are not in season. Preservation technology, artificial methods of ripening vegetables and fruits (carbide powder, for instance) and the late ripening crop varieties help to make seasonal fruits and vegetables available all the year round. We are trying to beat nature and are quite willing to pay more money for poorer quality of foodstuff, that, too, to eat foods that are off season. It does not make any sense to me.

Every region in India is a storehouse of several indigenous varieties of fruits, vegetables and pulses. When one buys local produce, one preserves the genetic biodiversity too. There are more than 50 varieties of *rajma* grown in India and we need to preserve this biodiversity by incorporating varied foods in our diets.

Eating local has other advantages besides the freshness and better nutritional content. The greater the distance that the food travels to reach the plate, the higher will be the carbon emissions due to transportation. Greater wastage of food also occurs during transportation and processing.

Packaged Foods and the Pitfalls

The easy availability of a wide variety of packaged foods and the convenience of preparation are strong temptations for the parent. These foods are cleverly advertised as healthy, thus making the task of well-meaning parents doubly difficult. Children also happily take to these foods, thereby simplifying the meal routines. As a result, we eat less of the locally grown seasonal and fresh foods these days. The hectic schedule of parents is another reason why resorting to packaged foods has become common.

A new book titled *Salt Sugar Fat: How the Food Giants Hooked Us* is an in-depth analysis of how food-manufacturing companies are responsible for the many health problems we face today. Once children develop the taste for such foods, the addiction is hard to overcome and worse than that of marijuana. Not everyone recognizes the salt, sugar and fat addiction to be as threatening and insidious.

Biting into an apple or having an orange is better than drinking any exotic variety of packaged juice. Fresh corn is a better choice than cornflakes. I want to leave a lasting message that there is *no substitute for fresh food.* If one does happen to consume packaged food for any reason, it becomes important to regulate the portion size. A packet of roasted soya sticks devoured hungrily in the mistaken belief that one is eating healthy is a problem, as this is only slightly better than polishing off a packet of regular chips!

Growing Concerns

The use of pesticides as well as the practice of adding colours to make the food more appealing is a matter of great concern today. Newspapers and magazines run several articles alerting us to these trends. The bright red apples and the suspiciously green *parwals* and peas are cases in point. The use of chemicals to hastily ripen fruits is a reality. Milk, too, has not been spared and we have to worry about adulterated milk as well. No wonder there is an inclination towards going organic!

Strong Case for Organic Foods?

In the past there have been conflicting reports on the real value of organically grown foodstuff. The UK Food Standards Agency (FSA) in 2009 found that there was no significant nutritional benefit offered by the consumption of organic food. However, a research paper in the *British Journal of Nutrition 2014* reveals a different picture. It cites 50 per cent lower levels of metal contaminants (mercury, lead and cadmium) and significantly higher levels (69 per cent) of antioxidants in organically grown crops.

Organically grown foodstuff scores over regular food in terms of fewer pesticide residues, thereby making it a healthier option. This aspect of organic foods is a common finding in all studies, new and old, and makes them superior to conventionally grown foods. Although organic food is grown without synthetic pesticides, there may always be some level of contamination due to exposure to air, packaging material and so on.

I am often asked to explain why organically grown plants have more beneficial compounds. This is because such plants have a stronger natural defence mechanism to fend off a wide range of pests and insects. The greater the amount of defensive compounds produced by the plant, the more benefits it has for us.

There is a higher concentration of vitamins and minerals (Vitamin C, iron, magnesium and phosphorus) found in organic foods. While growing regular foodstuffs, nitrogen fertilizers are used to drive the yield up and produce larger fruits. While these fruits may be juicier and larger in general, the concentration of vitamins diminishes.

Another advantage of organic produce is its **shelf life.** Higher levels of antibacterial compounds are produced in organically grown foods to ward off pests, which is why they keep better.

Don't Get Misled

Do keep in mind that the label of organic food does not necessarily classify the food as healthy! Junk foods (foods that are very low in nutritive worth) could also be made from organic products. For instance, a bag of French fries could be made with organically grown potatoes.

Therefore, it may not make too much sense to go in for organic foods without a clear understanding.

If organic food is not available, there is no reason to fret.

- Eat a variety of fruits and vegetables not just for imbibing diverse nutrients but also to limit exposure to any one type of pesticide residue.
- It is possible to eliminate pesticide residues to a large extent by proper washing techniques.

The alarming increase in incidents of tapeworm infections, even in vegetarians, necessitates attention to this significant aspect of healthy eating – washing – which is dealt with in another section (see Chapter 6: *Washing and Storage*).

To conclude, it is clear that organic produce is superior to the conventional variety. But here is a fact that needs to be highlighted: Those who eat more fruits and vegetables are healthier even if they do not eat organic. Thus, the primary aim is to eat more of this category of foods. There is absolutely no sense in restricting the consumption of fruits and veggies if one is not able to procure organic produce. Compromising on quantity and variety in order to eat organic does not make sense.

Here are some of the recognized organic-food certification agencies in India that you could look out for:

1. **Natural Organic Certification Association**
   www.nocaindia.com
2. **Bureau Veritas Certification India Pvt. Ltd**
   www.bureauveritas.co.in
3. **Ecocert SA**
   www.ecocert.in
4. **Control Union Certifications**
   www.controlunion.in
5. **International Resources for Fairer Trade**
   www.irft.org
6. **IMO Control Pvt. Ltd**
   www.imo.ch
7. **Skal International (India)**
   www.skal.org
8. **Aditi Organics Certification Pvt. Ltd**
   www.aditicert.net
9. **APOF Organic Certification Agency (AOCA)**
   www.aoca.in
10. **Indian Organic Certification Agency (INDOCERT)**
    www.indocert.org
11. **Lacon Quality Certification Pvt. Ltd**
    www.laconindia.com
12. **Rajasthan Organic Certification Agency (ROCA)**
    www.rajasthankrishi.gov.in

13. **OneCert Asia Agri Certification Pvt. Ltd**
www.onecertasia.in
14. **SGS India Pvt. Ltd**
www.sgs.com
15. **Uttaranchal State Organic Certification Agency (USOCA)**
www.usoca.org
16. **FoodCert India Pvt. Ltd**
www.foodcert.in
17. **Vedic Organic Certification Agency**
www.vediccertification.com
18. **PGS Organic India Council**
www.pgsorganic.in

Grocery Shopping: Pointers

1. Never shop when hungry to rule out impulsive purchases.
2. Always make a list so that you pick up only what you require.
3. Go for the unflavoured variants of foods such as cereals, yogurt, tea and so on. Such foods give you the freedom to add natural flavours of your choice. The more fancy the product, the higher its price and, usually, the lower its nutritional worth.
4. Stock up on some frozen fruits and veggies so that you can stir up a nutritious meal on lazy days (instead of going for the packaged foods).
5. Look into your grocery bag before you leave the store. If half your bag contains fruits and veggies, one-quarter nuts, seeds and healthy oils, and the rest whole grains and legumes, consider it a successful trip.

[5]

Reading Food Labels

In these times of micro-information, food labels have become very important. The purpose of the labels is to help consumers gain some insight into the nutritional claims that are made, which is why reading labels correctly is important. For instance, we have become wary of fats these day and do make an effort to stay away from fried foods. We try and find fat-free products in the market, which are, of course, available in abundance. Do you not pick up baked chips thinking they would have less fat? Often, what is promised is not delivered, especially as far as low fat and low sugar claims are concerned. Read on to know whether we are actually getting what the label claims.

The information displayed on the label should be able to help you to make appropriate food choices. Labels list ingredients, including additives, as well as information about the nutrition content, such as fat and proteins. They also indicate the 'use by' date and give critical information to people with food allergies.

In India, there are no strict guidelines that govern the details and authenticity of the information on food labels. If at all we get to see labels on our food products, they tend to be incomplete or mysterious. If you don't know what's in it, should you be eating it?

At times, the nutritional information provided to consumers is slanted so as to make it appealing. One of my clients happily reported to me that her child's favourite cola company had brought down the cola's calorie content. What had really happened was that the company had decided to advertise the calorie content a little more cleverly! Instead of listing the total number of calories in the drink, they decided upon a rather small serving size (100ml) and then told us how many calories that serving size contained. So it was not that the calorie content of the beverage had been reduced, but the information was tweaked so as to make it more attractive. For instance, companies will claim that their drink contains 40 calories per 100ml serving size whereas the actual size of the drink will be much larger and the total number of calories far greater. Colas are almost always only available in 250ml, 500ml or larger sizes, and not in serving sizes as small as 100ml (which is only half a cup!). And we sure know that there aren't many kids who are likely to put down the beverage after drinking only half a cup.

In order to convey the right information, the nutritional content should be calculated according to the real serving size. Which is why learning to read and understand labels is crucial.

'Neelanjana,' said my friend, bursting with enthusiasm, 'my son has decided to go on a diet. I have thrown out the packets of chips, *namkeens*, all those devilish temptations, and stocked up on fruits, roasted *namkeens* for the salt craving, and granola bars and multigrain biscuits in lieu of sweets.' I wished I could have shared her excitement, but the dietician in me could only see the hidden calories and the excess salt and sugar (in the form of corn syrup, dextrose, malt, maltodextrin and more).

For instance, one food brand claims that their product is made with whole grain. What is not evident to the consumer is that there is 10.4g sugar per serving of 30g of this wholegrain food. Such a proportion of sugar in a product means that one-third of the food is actually just sugar. Can such a food be labelled healthy even if it is prepared from whole grain? I only wish we got what the labels really claim.

Likewise, the word 'natural' can also be deceptive. Although one serving of a granola bar contains oats, honey and raisins, it also contains more sugar than traditional glazed doughnuts! In such a case, it may be better to switch to doughnuts for breakfast! Similarly, a fruit drink for children may be fortified with vitamins A, B, and C, but contains 18g sugar in 19g of the powder! Such brands should drop all claims of being 'healthy'. A single pack of instant noodles may have salt on the ingredients list but does not mention the amount in the nutrition information label. How healthy can this be if the recommended daily intake of salt is exceeded? One packet of noodles may load your child with more than half of the salt that he or she needs in a day.

Ambiguous food labelling has made matters tough. People make conscious choices regarding what they eat, yet they do not seem to derive the desired health benefits. This is because health claims on many food products are misleading, based on flimsy science. For these reasons, choosing the right healthier alternatives among packaged foods is difficult.

In such a scenario, understanding food labels has become a daily necessity and a few guidelines can help us in our everyday choices.

The First Ingredient

It is not going to be of much help if the healthy ingredient that you are seeking is the twentieth on the ingredients list. For instance, we all know that chocolate is not on the list of forbidden foods anymore, despite being relatively high on saturated fat. But, to derive benefit from chocolate products, choose products that list cocoa or chocolate liquor as the first ingredient. Sugar should not be one of the first two items listed if one is looking for a healthy version of chocolate.

The ingredient list is supposed to be made in order of weight. Thus the ingredient listed first is used in the largest amount in that product. The descending order of predominance by weight is the prescribed way of listing ingredients.

Milk Additives: A Top Favourite

We add different powders to milk, thinking that they are fortifying the milk with beneficial nutrients. Grand health claims as part of marketing tactics do not always have any meaning in scientific terms. For instance, fortification with 'EnVita' nutrients has no meaning in scientific terms. This is an example of how consumers are being overloaded with information that they do not understand. Also, remember that such powders are high on sugar and malt. Therefore, cocoa or fruits added to milk are better choices than such additives.

Advertisements could also be misleading for consumers. Not just children but adults also get taken in by clever advertising. For instance, there is a client of mine who always had a thing about height. A tall person has a personality advantage, was her unshakeable belief. So when she came upon an advertisement for an additive to milk, which claimed to make children grow tall, she quickly got her son on to it. However, her son grew up to be of average height.

Health Food Drinks (HFD) could contain malt and sugar in good amounts. Watch out for them! I would also like to make my readers aware of some common marketing gimmicks that get you to believe that a product may be of special value.

Marketing Tactics

1. **Wholegrain:** The law does not specify the precise quantity of whole grain that a product should contain before using the label 'wholegrain'. Taking advantage of such slack laws, food manufacturers get away with more refined flour and very marginal quantities of whole grain in what they label wholewheat bread, flours and biscuits.

2. **Multigrain:** This indicates that many grains are being used. However, if these multi (many) grains are used after they have been refined, not much benefit will accrue

from the product in spite of it being made with many types of grain.

3 **Real fruit:** Candies, beverages and many snacks that claim to be made with fruit contain only very small quantities of highly processed fruit juice or extract. Some products use concentrated juice as a sweetener instead of sugar so that they can make a claim of a 100% fruit product. However, this is not a very healthy alternative. The reality is that the so-called healthy fruit juice may actually turn out to be very high on simple sugars and calories, and not so healthy, after all. Do read the amount/percentage of real fruit in the product. 'Fruit flavour' does not have the benefit of fruit nutrients. Similarly 'juice drinks', 'fruit-flavoured drinks' or 'juice blends' have negligible fruit and more of added sugar. One has to also remember that juices can never match the fibre of whole fruit even though some juices claim to retain the pulp in them.

4 **Cholesterol-free food** should have < 2mg cholesterol and < 2g saturated fat and trans fat combined. Low-fat foods are not necessarily low-calorie, or free from fat. Naturally, such foods may lead to weight gain if large amounts are consumed. This kind of clever advertising may be seen for biscuits, for instance, which use the word 'thin' to signify a low-fat product, which is not really so.

On labels, the description 'light' could indicate either one-third/half the calories or half the amount of fat compared to the regular product. It could also mean that the product is lighter in colour and texture. This aspect should be specified on the label.

5 **Sugar-Free:** Only if a product contains < 5g sugar per serving.

6 **Trans fats:** The consumption of this kind of fat increases LDL (bad fat) levels. Processed foods can easily pass off as trans fat free if they contain <0.5g trans fat per serving. If a child is consuming large amounts of processed foods, the tally of trans fats could add up to quite a bit. The WHO recommendation says that children should not imbibe more than 2.6g of trans fats in a day.

One of my clients, who by now is a stickler for reading food labels, scans nearly every 'junk' item that she picks up at the grocery store for trans fats. Like most young people today, she loves her mug of hot chocolate every evening. She thought she had made the perfect choice by opting for a brand whose label clearly read '0 grams trans fats'. Alas, when she brought this product to my notice, I realized that the ingredients list mentioned hydrogenated coconut oil – which happens to contain trans fats (like all hydrogenated oils)!

It is important to make a distinction between '0 grams of trans fats' and '0% trans fats'. Often, bags of chips read '0 grams trans fats', but that is likely to mean that it is an amount less than 1g: for instance, 0.5 or 0.9g. These labels, thus, are quite misleading, and should be examined carefully since trans fats do add up in the long run, especially when such products are consumed regularly and in fairly large quantities.

6 **Fresh:** Such a claim can only be made for a food which is raw and has not been processed. However, this label is frequently used without any basis.

7 **Healthy:** Such a product should have low fat, low saturated fat, have <60mg cholesterol, not more than 360–480mg sodium, adequate iron, calcium, protein and fibre. As you can see, this is not an easy claim to make, yet 'healthy' foods flood the market.

Be Alert to Labels: A Few Facts

- 1 tablespoon of ketchup has 4g sugar.
- 1 cup pasta sauce has 20g sugar.
- Even some types of salted chips have over 6g of sugar in a 100g pack.
- 35 per cent of the calories of a veggie burger and 47 per cent of the calories of a non-veg burger are from fat. A typical meal at a fast-food outlet contains 47–51 per cent of the calorie requirement for the entire day!

Quite clearly, if one were on a diet mostly comprising processed foods, there would be no room for dessert on the menu!

DECEPTIVELY 'HEALTHY'

FOODS	WHAT COULD BE WRONG
Salads	Dressings; processed meat, like bacon
Fat-free foods	May not be low-calorie. Usually high on sodium and sugar
Energy bars	White flour, sugar, saturated fat. Usually low on fibre
Smoothie	Frozen yogurt bereft of beneficial bacteria. Added fruit may be in the form of juice
Cereal packs	Sugar-coated and frosted ones

For this reason it is vital to have tasty alternatives to the junk food that children crave.

A few important reminders:

- Don't assume that low-fat or 'diet' food has lower calories.
- Substitution of sugar with fat is common in low-fat food products.

Good to Be Connected

Parents tend to look only at the dark side of the Internet as children tend to go overboard with computer time. However, there is also a good side to this kind of connectivity. The ability to seek out more information, in fact, is actually forcing top food manufacturers to reconsider the ingredients, labelling and processing of their products. A 17-year-old from Mississippi, US, started a campaign that forced a sports drink manufacturer to remove the harmful ingredient – brominated vegetable oil (BVO) – from its product. BVO is a synthetic chemical added to soft drinks and sports drinks to provide a fruity flavour. It has now been replaced with an alternative natural additive, largely due to this teenager's efforts.

Social media brought to light the fact that azodicarbonamide (a chemical found in shoes and yoga mats) was found in bread used by a reputed fast-food chain. This chemical was added to increase the volume and improve the texture of the bread. The chain had to phase out the unnecessary chemical and today their website declares that their bread is free from azodicarbonamide.

A very popular chocolate brand is replacing its widely used food dyes with safer alternatives as a result of consumer demands. Yet another chocolate brand is replacing one of its food dyes with an alternative made from seaweed.

The nutrition label should help the consumer in making an informed choice. Some ingredient names may not give an indication of their chemical makeup. For instance, corn syrup, concentrated fruit juice sweetener and so on are all forms of sugar. Baking soda, baking powder and MSG, all have has sodium present in them.

One of the new trends in marketing is to promote the not-so-healthy foods in smaller and less expensive packets. Mini packets of *namkeens* have flooded shops and what seems to be happening is that the small packaging reduces guilt and propagates unhealthy snacking more frequently. So, it has been noticed that the total consumption of the unhealthy product goes up. One does need to be conscious of miscalculations in such cases.

Food Labels: The Fine Print

It's not always easy to figure out what's what on a label. Here are some examples that will clarify the issues that concern parents and kids.

Take the instance of this product in which 1 serving provides 140 calories and there are 5 servings in the pack. So consuming the whole packet provides 700 calories, which is one-third or 33 per cent of the recommended calorie intake for a 12-year-old boy (total calorie needs are 2,190.) Not many kids are able to resist the temptation of polishing off the entire packet once opened!

As a prototype, take nacho crisps. Now let us look at how many servings a packet contains. The serving per pack/

container is an important detail to be noted. I would like to alert you to the fact that many packets mention the total number of servings in the bag in not very precise terms such as 'about 5' or 'approx. 5', which may really be an underestimated amount. The total weight of the product will help us make this simple calculation. For example, if the net weight of the packet reads 170g, but at the same time it mentions that one serving size is 30g, then you should be wary of the label reading 'approx. 5 servings'. This is one of the most common ways for brands to cover up for an evident discrepancy of 20g (in this case).

Decoding Food Labels: A Few Pointers

1 **How to Understand Values for Fats:** Looking at percentages rather than amounts gives you a better idea of how much fat a product contains. Unfortunately, most of the Indian food companies do not represent food values in terms of percentage on the label. In such cases, we have to make an estimate based on the amount stated in grams.

Many food companies quote ridiculously small serving sizes so that the product appears to be a healthy one. When you open up a bag of chips, how likely are you to stop eating after just 30g – a typically quoted serving size – of it (just 15–20 pieces)?

For instance, a bag of masala peanuts states that 100g of the product (half of the packet) contains 610 calories. The quantity of fat present in half the packet is 50g (provides 450 calories). Thus, 450 of the total 610 calories come from fat, which is a whopping 73 per cent. Dietary recommendations are that only 30 per cent of the calories should come from fat. This means that such a snack is not something that you should opt for very frequently. In order to keep fat intake in check, choose foods that have 3g or less of fat per 100 calories.

Watching out for the type of fat is also important. Check values of saturated fat and trans fats on the label.

A popular brand of milk chocolate may state that the total fat in a mid-sized bar is 37 per cent, but the saturated fat content is 60 per cent! The recommendation is to limit saturated fats to 8–10% of the total fat in the product. Trans fats are not desirable and should ideally be avoided altogether.

2 **Sodium values:** You may perhaps know that many naturally occurring foods have sodium present in it. Thus, the body really does not need much of added salt except in special conditions. You may find it intriguing that almost all the salted snacks manufactured in India do not even mention the sodium salt values on their packs.

Many of these packs are actually loaded with salt, containing over 20 per cent of Daily Value or DV (see box: *Nutrient Value Indicators in Products*, page 108), which is excessive considering the many packs that kids devour. Some chips contain 14.7 per cent sodium per serving, which again makes it a significant source of the same. Go for foods that contain less than 400mg sodium per serving.

3 **Protein Values:** Ideally, snacks for children should contain a reasonable amount of protein (15–20 per cent of the total calories). Protein is important for growth and muscle development in children. Granola bars are touted as great snack options for children. Did you know that many of these contain as little as 3g protein in one whole bar? Thus, when such bars are consumed as a snack option, one has to ensure that protein needs are met adequately from other

sources during the day. This is a good time to point out the fact that that inadequate protein intake can slow down the metabolism of carbohydrates too.

4 **Total Carbohydrates:** The body needs energy, which it derives mainly from carbohydrates. If a snack provides 10 per cent of the calories from carbs, it is a good thing, but paying attention to the source of carb is just as important. Whole grain is preferable over sugar as a source of carbohydrate. It is also important to remember that if the snack has loads of salt and fat accompanying the healthy carb, it will negate the healthy aspect of the carb. You may notice on some food labels the mention of '1 carbohydrate choice/serve'. One 'choice' or 'serve' of carbohydrate is 15g, which provides 60 calories (1g carbohydrate provides 4 calories).

5 **Sugars:** We do not need simple sugars in large amounts. When looking out for snacks that are healthy, go for ones low on sugar (sugar should be 5 per cent of the total calories required in a day) Simple sugars are added to snacks, candies, bars and so on, and should be consumed only in limited amounts. Many of the chocolates imply that they are healthy because of the high cocoa content (50 per cent and above) but have large amounts of added sugars. One bar of a commonly available brand of dark chocolate contains nearly half its weight as sugar (38g in a bar of 80g.). Even in granola bars, the amount of sugar is quite high (13g of sugar present in a bar of 35g, which means that 37 per cent is just sugar).

6 **Vitamins and Minerals:** Check the food label to see if the food is a rich source of any of these. A granola bar contains calcium 2% DV and iron 2% DV. It does not contain

any significant amounts of Vitamin A and Vitamin C. If a food item only provides such minuscule amounts of important nutrients, it would be wise to switch to healthier alternatives. Try some of the snack options in the *Recipes* section.

7 **Fibre:** If the product has < 10% of DV, then it is quite obviously not a significant source of fibre.

NUTRIENT VALUE INDICATORS IN PRODUCTS

- 5 per cent or less of a nutrient: The food is a poor source of that nutrient.
- 10–20 per cent of your daily recommended amount of a nutrient: The food is a reasonable source of that nutrient.
- More than 20 percent of the nutrient: The food is high on that nutrient.
- The Percent Daily Value %DV) on the label is a guide to the nutrients in one serving of food. It is useful only for comparing one food with another. It is not useful for assessing your nutrient targets as it is mistakenly believed to show.

Recap

- The ***listing order of the ingredients*** indicates a great deal about the product. Sugar, oil or salt as the first few ingredients definitely reflect poorly on the nutritional quality.
- A product with many chemical names indicates that it is highly processed. In general, the longer the ingredient list, the less natural the food product is likely to be.
- Junk food will have calories from sugar and fat and will be devoid of other nutrients such as vitamins, minerals and fibre.

[6]

Washing and Storage

Here I am going to add one more story to the endless *saas-bahu* sagas! I had a daughter-in-law as my client, who was having arguments with her mother-in-law because she was convinced that her child's frequent bouts of diarrhoea were because of the faulty washing practices in her husband's home. Little wonder that the mother-in-law was mightily offended. I was able to restore harmony by giving them some advice, without hurting anyone.

Washing practices vary from home to home. Each household vouches for following the safest and best practices to maintain hygiene. Here, I am listing the advice that I gave that family and give to all my clients.

Washing Fresh Produce

1 Proper washing of fruits and vegetables is necessary to remove dirt, bacteria and harmful pesticides. Ideally, it is best to wash fruits and vegetables just before use. In fact, the risk of cross-contamination is minimized if the product is thoroughly washed just before cutting or peeling. Washing produce before storing promotes bacterial growth and speeds up spoilage. However, if you choose to wash before storing, dry well with a paper or cloth towel before refrigeration.

2 Thorough rinsing of fresh produce under running water is an effective way to remove not only dirt and bacteria, but also residual pesticides.

3 Another effective method is to soak raw fruits and vegetables in hydrogen peroxide solution and then rinse off with running water. This procedure removes traces of bacteria and pesticides. The soaking process should be done in a clean utensil rather than in the sink. The drain area of the sink usually harbours many microbes, so avoid using the sink for holding water and soaking vegetables and fruits.

The new generation of fruit and vegetable washes contain malic acid, lactic acid, citric acid and aloe vera leaf juice powder. Such solutions get rid of *E.coli*, Listeria and Salmonella bacteria. They have no aftertaste and the time required for contact with produce is just 30 seconds. These solutions should be available in India soon.

Here's a word of caution regarding commercial fruit and vegetable washes. The safety of the chemical residues of these products left on the skin of the food has not yet been evaluated and their effectiveness has not been tested and standardized. Therefore, for the time being, it is safer to avoid commercial fruit and vegetable washes that are available in the market.

The washing procedure varies depending on the type and the characteristics of the produce.

- Leafy green vegetables are difficult to clean. The proper way is to immerse the leaves in a bowl of cold water for a few minutes. To this, add vinegar (half cup white vinegar to 1 cup water). Then, rinse with plain water to reduce bacterial contamination.
- Remove the outermost layer of leaves of cabbage before washing and cooking to reduce pesticide residues.
- It is a good idea to use a vegetable brush to clean the outer skin of those vegetables/fruits that have a rough, netted surface like bitter gourd, melon, carrot and potatoes. While washing, cleaning with a brush for 5–10 seconds is effective for root vegetables with a rough outer peel, such as yam and sweet potato.
- Vegetables such as cauliflower, broccoli and green beans should be soaked in lukewarm salt water (2 per cent) for 2 minutes before cooking. This really means one should add 20g/4 tsp salt to 1 litre of water, which helps to wash away the pesticides present in the food.
- Do not use detergent and bleach solutions to clean the food as the porous skin of fruits and vegetables could absorb some of them and render the food unfit for consumption.
- Washing of meats, poultry and eggs is not recommended before storage. In fact, washing before storage helps bacteria to spread, and the risk of cross

contamination goes up. They should be washed just before use.

The next aspect of healthy eating focuses on the storage of food. There is no denying that fresh food tastes best (though there are some exceptions in the category of dals – Makhani dal tastes better after it is stored in the fridge overnight!). But these days, eating fresh produce is considered a luxury, so it is all the more important to store food in a way so that the important nutrients are not lost.

Storing Food

The relevance of storage of food is becoming increasingly important in our lives. We now stock all kinds of raw, packaged and cooked foods at home. All of these need care and monitoring when you store them.

Certain foods can be stored for reasonably long periods of time without being refrigerated. Grains should be stored in dry jars at room temperature.

Foodstuffs such as sugar, salt and lentils can also be stored for long periods at room temperature.

Some veggies and fruits are better off without refrigeration. These include melon, sweet potato, garlic, onion and pumpkin.

The more processed the food, the greater the care it needs while storing. For example, flours are very prone to infestation by mites. Storing them in a plastic bag is not a good idea as mites can easily make tiny holes in the plastic wrapper to contaminate the product.

- It is far more prudent to store flour in the freezer for 48 hours and then transfer it to an airtight/food-grade plastic/steel container. This practice will inactivate any mites that may be present in it without being visible. Bay leaves added to the flour will also keep bugs away.

- For storing rice, too, add bay leaves/dried neem leaves to keep the mites out.

Refrigerating Food

Are you surprised to find that tomatoes freeze in the fridge during the winter, or that food products go rancid despite being in the fridge? A little information on appropriate refrigeration methods comes in handy.

For instance, it is vital to know that the temperature setting of the fridge should remain constant throughout all seasons (summer and winter). The storage temperature plays a role in preserving the nutrient content of the food. It is not enough to store the food in the fridge and believe that it is in good hands! Temperature regulation is all-important. It should be maintained during all seasons at <40°F (4°C) for the fridge and at 0°F (-18°C) for the freezer).

If the ice cream in the freezer is not solid, it means that the freezer is not set at the right temperature.

Refrigeration should not be taken as the licence to store food indefinitely! Spinach will lose most of its nutrients after one week. Refrigeration is good but works well for some days. Therefore, it is smart not to buy too much at once.

- Different foods need to be stored differently. Leafy vegetables can be stored in cloth bags or in a damp muslin cloth. However, avoid the use of plastic to store herbs for long periods in the fridge as the plastic tends to absorb the natural compounds from the herbs and the herbs may no longer taste great.

- Cut/peeled/cooked fruits and vegetables should be covered and stored in the fridge preferably in airtight containers but not for long periods. Uncovered food storage is a bad practice. Not only does it facilitate bacterial multiplication but it also leads to loss of nutrients.
- Do not store raw and cooked food together. It is best to store raw foods on the bottom shelf so that the juices that leak do not contaminate the rest of the food stored.
- Once opened, food cans should not be used for storing the food in the fridge. The food in the can should be transferred to another container immediately after opening the can as the metal (tin/aluminium) may leach into the can's contents. Once the can is opened, transfer the contents into a covered bowl or any other appropriate storage container.
- Very hot food should not be stored in the fridge. Ideally, it should be cooled quickly and then refrigerated within an hour.
- Always store raw meats away from the ready-to-eat foods. Fresh meats and poultry may be refrigerated for up to a period of two days, and sausages and ground meats for one to two days. After this period, the meats should be frozen either raw or after cooking. Eggs can be stored for 3–5 weeks in the fridge. To test the freshness of the egg, put it in a pan of water. If the egg sinks, it is fresh. If it floats, it is stale.
- Remember the 'two-hour rule' for items that need refrigeration. Any food that requires refrigeration

should not be left at room temperature for longer than two hours. However, in case the room temperature is above 32°C, the food should be refrigerated within an hour. Never leave such foods at room temperature for a longer period.

- One is unlikely to find cooking oil in the fridge in most homes. Nevertheless, this remains the best way to store it! Once the pack of cooking oil has been opened, the most practical thing is to take out the amount of oil one requires in the day and store the rest of the packet in the fridge.
- Nuts and oilseeds, such as flaxseeds, are also best refrigerated after opening the packs. If such oilseeds are ground, spoilage occurs even faster. It would be best to store these items in the fridge if the amount is to last for over two weeks. For longer storage, nuts and oilseeds could also be frozen in airtight containers. Alternately, if this is not available, cling film or aluminium foil should be used not just for halting the contamination but also to prevent the oxidation that occurs when the food is exposed to air.

PRESERVING AND STORING GREENS

The only way to store green leaves in the fridge for long periods is by cooking them briefly, i.e., by blanching. Blanching stops the enzymatic process that makes the leaves turn black and, at the same time, does not take away nutrients. It preserves the colour, flavour and texture of the leaves. Follow this procedure.

- Wash the leafy vegetable thoroughly.
- Boil water in a pan, add the leaves to the boiling water and let them remain in the boiling water for 20 seconds.
- Drain the blanched leaves in a sieve/colander and plunge into a bowl of ice-cold water.
- Remove and squeeze the water out of the leaves. This may cause the leaves to clump up, but do not worry. Drain excess water and pack.
- Label and freeze. Labelling is important as all leaves may look similar after blanching.

The above-mentioned method can be used for most leafy vegetables. For tougher leaves such as those of radish, the blanching time should be 30 seconds. In the case of non-leafy veggies, such as corn, the blanching time would be one minute. Beans and beans and broccoli require two minutes.

More about Veggie Preservation and Storage

I visit the Sunday vegetable market not just for the routine of buying vegetables for the week but also for the sheer love of feasting my eyes on the fresh produce. This sometimes compels me to buy more than the required amount. With such buying emerges the problem of lugging it home and storing it. Once I reach home, I get into the act of arranging them in the fridge in such a way that it looks neat, colourful and picture perfect in the vegetable bin of the fridge. In order to achieve this, I follow some rules that I would recommend:

Blanching: Blanch green leafy veggies unless they are to be used within a day or so. Blanching has another byproduct advantage! It reduces the astringent taste of the leaves, thus making it easier for children to like them!

Freezing: Shopping and freezing the same day has the advantage of preserving many of the vitamins that decrease with storage time. Wash, peel if required and cut uniformly. Take double the volume of water and bring to a boil. Add the prepared veggies, turn into a sieve or colander and drain the water. Cool and store in metal containers or freezer-safe plastic bags.

Purée: Extra tomatoes could be puréed and frozen for quick use. Similarly a paste of garlic/ginger could be made and bottled.

Packaged Foods

When buying packaged food, besides the price and the weight, it is important to look at two dates: The date of manufacture and the date of expiry.

The mention of the 'Best before' date is to indicate the period of the best flavour and quality. It is not a safety date.

You may find the 'Use by' date on some products. This is the recommended date for the use of the product. It is by this date that the product remains at its peak quality. This date is determined by the manufacturer.

Many products indicate the shelf life of the product, which is calculated from the date of manufacture.

[7]

Cooking and Cookware

One would naturally like to opt for a method of preparation that results in the least loss of nutrients. Very often, it is possible to tweak the usual cooking style to reap a huge advantage.

It is well known that extended periods of cooking can destroy many nutrients and thus reduce the food value. One can maximize nutritional benefit by adopting the following steps while cooking.

- It is better to cut food into bigger chunks rather than very small pieces.
- Avoid peeling foods as much as possible. However, if you must peel, it would be better to first cook with the peel and then remove it. Adopting such a method ensures that the nutrients present in the peel get assimilated

into the food and the prepared dish. I would suggest using this method for potatoes, zucchini, pumpkin and similar vegetables.

- Do not overcook veggies. Let them remain a little crisp. More nutrients remain intact this way.
- Always cover the container while boiling or cooking. This not only reduces the cooking time but also preserves nutrients.

Although everyone uses the microwave for heating food, there is a lot of scepticism regarding this practice. It is not harmful in the way that it is feared to be. In fact, microwave cooking, if done properly (in the correct utensils, with minimum water), can actually preserve nutrients better. For instance, microwaved spinach retains almost all its folate as opposed to stove-cooked spinach.

Therefore, reworking some of the cooking practices can reap a host of nutritional benefits! Choose to bake, grill, steam and sauté foods, as these are great methods of cooking.

The following cooking practices should be kept in mind when cooking pulses:

- Soaking pulses in boiling water overnight before pressure cooking shortens the cooking time and enhances the quality of the cooked product.
- If one is short on time, here is a quick method that can be used. Boil the pulses in water for two minutes, then soak for an hour and cook again.
- Soaking pulses in salted water is helpful.
- Addition of tamarind while cooking pulses helps retain some nutrients, particularly the B vitamins and calcium.

- Addition of cooking soda to pulses (sodium bicarbonate) may be a popular practice, but it should be discouraged as it causes the loss of B vitamins.
- Flatulence that may be caused by the consumption of pulses is reduced by soaking, pressure cooking, germination, fermentation and roasting.

There are many ways to cook foods and I believe that each one is best suited for one or the other kind of cooking technique.

Cooking Methods

Today, microwave ovens have become an indispensable and mandatory fixture in our homes. The biggest advantage is that microwave ovens reduce cooking time to almost a quarter. The benefit that one derives from the short cooking time is that of better preservation of heat-sensitive nutrients, particularly Vitamin C and beta-carotene. Thawing of frozen foods can be done in seconds using the microwave. Among all the methods of cooking, this one is best in terms of preservation of natural colours.

The disadvantage of this method, particularly sensed in Indian foods, is that there is no browning of the food as it cooks. It is also not feasible to boil eggs, or make Indian breads, such as chapattis, tandoori roti, puris and *bhaturas*. The short cooking time also does not allow the flavours to blend well in the food. Microwaves generally penetrate only 1–2 inches into the food, which may leave the core uncooked if the food item is bulky. This is advisable to cut sections of such foods, e.g., large potatoes, when cooking in the microwave.

It is important to be cautious when operating the microwave oven and also to use the right cookware. Glass without glazing, ceramic dishes and paper plates can be used for heating food in microwave ovens. For longer periods of cooking use heat-proof glass (ovenproof) dishes made of borosilicate. Avoid cookware with metal parts in lids and handles, and gold or silver trimmings. So far there is no conclusive evidence to support a link between the use of microwaves and the risk of cancer. I recommend that you use this method for greens and whenever you are short on time!

Once upon a time, pressure cookers were unheard of in the west. The popularity of this appliance has spread far and wide as it is a time- and fuel-saving method. As this method uses steam for cooking, the chances of the food burning is quite low. This method is best for tough-to-cook foods such as beans and whole lentils. However, when a pressure cooker is used, the chances of overcooking go up, especially when one is not familiar with the time–temperature connection. Overcooking tends to destroy the texture of foods.

In a convection oven, the food is cooked by dry heat and steam is generated from the food itself. Foods cooked by this method are crisp on the top and soft inside. The temperature maintained ranges between 120°C to 260°C. The advantage is that both the flavour and texture of the food improve.

A method synonymous with healthy cooking is steaming. As the veggies are not submerged in water while being steamed, they retain nutrients better. No oil is required. This method works best for cauliflower, carrots, broccoli, green beans, spinach and fish. It helps to retain both taste and colour to the maximum.

The easiest way to cook is to boil foods. For cooking a number of vegetables, blanching (a variant of boiling) is, in fact, recommended over boiling. When the water is at a full boil, add the veggies (for instance, green beans or broccoli), immerse briefly and remove. Blanching helps to preserve the crispness and flavour of vegetables effectively. Utilizing the water used for boiling/blanching veggies in soups and curries is a good idea. Simmering is a slow-cooking method that is good for root vegetables, such as yam and sweet potatoes, which require a longer cooking time. This method also boosts the carotene content several folds as opposed to steaming or frying.

A quick way to cook in a hot pan with a little oil is sautéing. It helps to retain nutrients and flavour as well as taste, and is suitable for tender veggies such as capsicum, onions and mushrooms. Remember to cut the veggies into bite-sized portions (not too large) so that the cooking is even.

Stir-frying is similar to sautéing. The difference is in the utensil used– a wok, which withstands a high temperature throughout the cooking process. Stir constantly to prevent burning. Use oil that tolerates high heat (canola/rice bran) and later add olive/peanut/sesame oil for flavour.

Place the vegetables on a baking dish, drizzle with vegetable oil and place in an oven at 400 °C. The high temperature caramelizes the sugar on the surface, making the vegetables crunchy and sweet. Voila, you have roast veggies!

Like roasting, grilling makes veggies crispy and sweet. Potatoes, onions, corn, chicken and peppers are suited for this technique. You could also grill by holding the vegetables with a pair of tongs over the fire on a gas stove.

Frying

Fats have a ubiquitous presence in food preparation and enhance the taste of food manifold. Among all the various ways in which fat is utilized in cooking, frying remains the most popular. In both shallow-frying and deep-frying, the fat is heated at above 165°C. Frying cooks the food quickly.

When choosing the oil for frying, keep the following points in mind:

- The fat should be able to withstand spoilage when it is exposed to air and water (water comes from the food and air/oxygen is present around us). Corn is more stable than soya whereas rapeseed is better than olive oil. In general, oils that have not been refined have better oxidative stability at high temperatures than the refined versions.
- The fat selected for frying should have a high smoking point. The smoking point is the point at which the fat begins to break down into different products. Different oils have varying heat tolerance. Coconut oil and butter have a lower smoking point as compared to safflower, soya, corn and canola.
  (a) While shallow-frying, the food is covered in fat but not completely. In this method, the advantage is that the amount of fat can be controlled as you keep adding it to the food as you go instead of submerging the food in oil as in deep-frying.
  (b) When deep-frying, food is totally submerged in oil and cooks uniformly on all sides. Within minutes,

the food absorbs the fat, the food surface gets dehydrated and flavour compounds are formed. Cooking is rapid, too, as the temperature ranges between 180°C–220°C. Generally, 5–10 per cent of the oil is absorbed by the food item.

While shallow-frying, it is up to you to control the amount of fat being utilized. If one is too liberal with the amount used, then the whole purpose of shallow-frying is defeated. A paratha may actually contain more oil than a puri if one is liberal with the fat when shallow-frying the paratha. (One may only be able to do some damage control by dabbing a paper napkin to soak the extra oil in the food!)

One can reduce oil usage while baking, too! Use parchment paper and aluminium foil to line the baking dish instead of spraying it with oil.

Do take note that leftover oil after frying should not be used for frying again. It would be best if the leftover oil is used for sautéing and low temperature cooking (vegetables, dal). Repeated cycles of frying causes harmful chemicals to be produced in the oil.

Here is one rough way of estimating if excess oil is being consumed at your home: While doing the dishes, do you notice a greasy film of oil on the plates? If yes, you could very well think about using less fat for cooking.

What is an Air Fryer? This is a relatively new device to hit the market and has become the talk of the town. As the name suggests, the frying is done by air instead of the use of fat. The food item is moistened with a thin layer of fat/oil. Circulating hot air at high speed cooks food quickly. This is a quick and healthy way to cook, but the equipment is expensive.

Fortunately, some of the other conventional cooking methods are just as effective in preparing healthy, tasty foods.

Utensils

It is not just the healthy ingredients that matter but also the utensils in which they are cooked. Choosing the right cooking utensil is a crucial factor in optimizing nutrition. The cookware could contribute to certain benefits because of how it interacts with the food.

Traditionally, Indians have been aware of the importance of utensils – iron *karahis* were used for cooking and copper vessels were used for drinking and storing water. Such practices made a lot of sense as iron utensils added to the nutritional content and the copper vessels had inherent anti-bacterial properties.

The hidden components of the cookware are likely to be present in the food that one is eating. This is why sometimes food stored in plastic bags starts smelling and tasting like plastic. The ions of the wrapping/cookware interact with the food.

Now, with the advent of the microwave, non-stick kitchenware and the increased use of plastics, one needs to know of the possible threats apart from the apparent strengths of using these products.

Stainless steel is relatively inert but develops 'hot-spots' when heated, resulting in uneven cooking. Triple-ply stainless steel is a better alternative as it has a layer of aluminium between the stainless steel layers. Aluminium is a better conductor of heat, but it should not come in direct contact with the food, especially with tomato-based foodstuff. Thus, this triple layering provides good conduction of heat and little reaction with food.

Newer ways to reap the benefit of aluminium's heat conduction without its harmful effects have also been worked out. Hard anodized cookware is one such safe alternative. The electro-chemical anodizing process locks in the base metal, which is aluminium, so that it cannot make its way into the food. The advantage is that it is also non-stick and scratch-resistant with good conduction properties.

Teflon-coated (non-stick) cookware is also very popular because we are becoming more and more particular about the amount of oil that we use while cooking. It is a recent finding that there is a link between high levels of perfluorinated compounds (widely used in non-stick cookware) and diabetes. It would be a good idea to use the safer aforementioned alternatives when it comes to choosing cookware.

It is also important to acknowledge that food packaging material is a matter of concern in this era of packaged food. The synthetic chemicals used in food packaging, including plastic bottles, cups and plates, leach into the food. Quite evidently, those who regularly eat out of plastic and melamine tableware are chronically exposed to low doses of chemicals (e.g., formaldehyde), which over a period of time can add up to a substantial toxic dose for the body to cope with.

Glass, stainless steel and ceramic are materials preferable to plastic for cooking and storing, and as tableware. And do remember to buy stainless-steel, reusable bottles rather than fancy-looking plastic ones for your child!

SECTION 4

EVERYDAY FOOD PLANNING

[8]

BREAKFAST

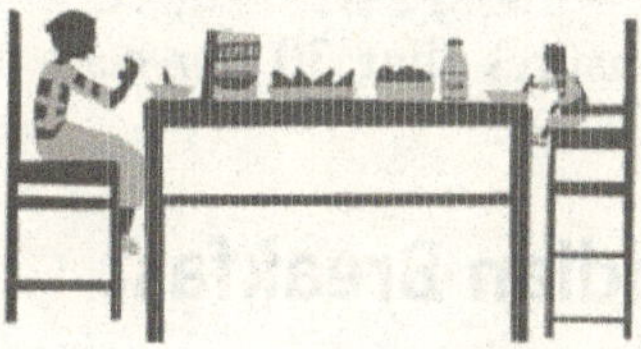

Up until I was a college student, my mother refused to let me leave home without my three-course consisting of porridge with milk, an egg and a seasonal fruit. My mother did not have any kind of training in nutrition, but she understood the importance of breakfast and balanced the nutrients beautifully in terms of carbohydrates, proteins, fats and vitamins.

Although the importance of breakfast has not diminished, such an elaborate breakfast is nearly impossible these days. Children have only a few minutes to spare between waking up and heading out the door for school.

I know of many children leaving home early in the morning without any food. The detrimental effects of skipping breakfast are reflected in a poor attention span and poor concentration ability among children at school. Of late, I have noticed that more and more kids do not like to drink any liquids early in the morning. Perhaps, the long bus/car ride to school makes them queasy. Here is a solution: Prepare Energy Bites or Sesame Bars (see *Recipes*) beforehand and let the child have that for breakfast, even if it is when they are on the move. Just 2 or 3 portions of the Energy Bites would be a wholesome way to start the day.

A healthy and wholesome breakfast reduces the child's desire to indulge in inappropriate food over the course of the day and ensures that 30 per cent of the day's diet remains sound.

The Great Indian Breakfast

For sheer variety and taste there is nothing that beats the Indian breakfast of parathas, *cheelas*, *tikkis*, *poha* and so on. Among all these foods, I think the idli scores over other Indian breakfast foods in terms of nutritive value. As a result of its popularity, the instant avatar (readymade powder mix) of idlis has become quite popular, too. I would like to reiterate that leaving home without breakfast is non-negotiable. So if you don't have the time to prepare breakfast, these readymade variants do not make for bad options.

The humble *upma* in the hands of Mumbai-born and New York-based celebrated chef, Floyd Cardoz, shot into culinary limelight very recently. His version made with semolina and mushroom won a prize of US$100,000!

Quite evidently, Indian breakfast foods are popular as well as wholesome. The use of traditional staples (amaranth, ragi) to prepare everyday Indian breakfast foods such as *dalia*, *upma* or *sewainyan* enhances their nutritional worth. These can give the new superfood quinoa stiff competition.

We know well that there is no substitute for a filling and nutritious breakfast. But our busy lifestyles and the morning rush for school and work prevent us from enjoying this meal. In fact, one tends to skip it.

Here's my take on breakfast:

- The secret of remaining sharp and energetic lies, to a great extent, in consuming a healthy breakfast. A healthy breakfast boosts brain power and provides adequate fuel to keep you going for the rest of the day. Kids need breakfast more than adults do as the meal affects learning, too. Their growing body and brain rely on regular intake of food.
- A good breakfast can empower your child to pass over junk food later during the day. Without a proper breakfast, distress signals are sent to the brain, which can trigger cravings and bingeing during the course of the day.

  Ideally, breakfast should comprise complex carbohydrates (whole grains), proteins (milk, yogurt, eggs) and a little fat. The small amount of fat ensures that one remains satisfied up until the next meal/snack. The value of fats in promoting satiety is well understood.

  However, a good breakfast need not be elaborate or time-consuming to prepare. For instance, the use of leftovers from the previous meal could be a viable option for breakfast, such as in a roti wrap or as a sandwich.
- Simplicity works best for breakfast. A fruit smoothie incorporates all the nutrients needed, yet it is quick

and easy to make. It is always a good idea to plan and prepare for breakfast the previous night. Once the adequacy of nutrients is ensured, it is important to add variety within the food group. For example, a bean cutlet could be replaced by a soya cutlet or a *matar ki tikki* as variants.

- We should not be caught in the rut of what we call 'breakfast foods'. In South–East Asia, the day begins with rice and noodles whereas in northern India a paratha is a must. Be flexible and creative with breakfast!

Besides the dishes mentioned above, here is a plan that could help you achieve healthy breakfast goals with ease. (See *Recipes*)

DAY 1: Yogurt with a bowl of granola
DAY 2: Garlic-Basil Bruschetta and fruit
DAY 3: Olive muffin and smoothie
DAY 4: Pancake and fruit
DAY 5: Mushrooms on toast with unsweetened orange juice
DAY 6: Lentil-stuffed roti roll with yogurt
DAY 7: All-dal idli (Powerpuff Idli) with chutney

Catering to the demands of working mothers and children who are on the go, a variety of breakfast cereals have flooded the market. They are being touted as very healthy foods. These products do make life easier, but the promised health benefit is under the scanner. Many of these cereals have more sugar in them than a French pastry. One such brand of cereal contains more than 10g of sugar in one serving of 30g. If kids consume such large quantities of sugar regularly, it is bound to turn them into sugar junkies.

If you have to choose a ready-to-eat cereal for children, definitely avoid the instant and flavoured variety. Also, choose a cereal pack that indicates that 100 per cent whole grain is used. I would like to mention that it is possible to prepare a mixture of cereals and nuts at home as well. Such a mix could be eaten as a snack, or could be added to milk or yogurt as a breakfast item (see *Recipes*).

Some foods seem to be universally seen on breakfast menus. Among them, oats, bread and eggs strike me as the most popular foods in today's scenario.

Oats

Groats, steel-cut and rolled oats are different kinds of oats with the same nutritional value. Instant oatmeal is a slightly processed form of oats that could contain excessive amounts of salt, sugar and other additives, which is why it is not the preferred choice.

Although the benefit of oats is usually attributed to its fibre content, we now know that there is more to oats than just fibre. AVE (avenanthramide), which is present uniquely in oats, has antioxidant, anti-inflammatory, anti-cancer and anti-irritant properties.

Eggs

Eggs have enjoyed immense popularity on the breakfast table for decades. Except for the missing carbohydrates, eggs contain all other important nutrients. They make a value addition to the diet of a growing child. A few years ago, research data linked eggs to heart disease and so their popularity plummeted. Fortunately, recent trials have exonerated eggs. Egg yolks, which were once considered akin to poison, are now known to contain a bounty of beneficial nutrients.

Each egg does contain 200mg cholesterol, but this cholesterol from eggs does not negatively impact blood cholesterol levels. It is the cholesterol that is made by the body itself (in the liver) in response to saturated and trans fats that is harmful. Eggs are relatively low in saturated fat, and they contain good quality protein, vitamins and minerals.

Very often, I meet vegetarians who cautiously exclude egg from their diet because they believe that it is a non-vegetarian food. I would urge the vegetarians to read this.

ARE EGGS A VEGETARIAN FOOD?

Yes, eggs are vegetarian food items. The eggs available in the market for consumption are the unfertilised kind, which are different from the ones that produce chicks (the fertilised ones). Therefore, we can categorize eggs as animal products (like milk) but not as non-vegetarian food items.

Boiled or poached eggs would be the simplest and healthiest way to consume them. In fact, 6–7 eggs a week should be mandatory for children. Eggs are memory and alertness boosters. To derive the alertness advantage, serve egg in the pre-exam meal to improve attentiveness.

Bread, milk and yogurt are common breakfast items all over the world and have been discussed earlier in Chapter 2.

[9]

Lunch and Dinner

Whenever I think of planning a lunch or dinner menu for kids, vegetables are topmost on my mind. This is because I find that feeding vegetables to children is the most challenging aspect of getting them to eat healthy. Their dislike for vegetables is not at all unusual. The number of taste buds in children is far more than in adults, so children are more sensitive to bitter tastes. This explains why as a child you may not have eaten papaya, but as an adult you enjoy it! My objective is to help you work around this issue and get your child to enjoy veggies and fruits.

My number one advice: Offer veggies and fruits as the first course to kids. This is when children are most likely to try what you offer them and, therefore, develop a liking for it.

So stock items like fruits, carrots and cucumber sticks at all times as they make easy 'grab and go' snacks. When initiating a solid diet for babies, start with vegetables that have milder flavours and gradually add more variety with time.

Spotlighting Salads

When your objective is to get children to eat healthy, salads served at lunch and dinner take up the prime position. According to the principles of Ayurveda, too, it is advisable to start with a salad.

Here is an interesting episode I wish to share with you. I was counselling a bemused mother. Her son, as a child, would prefer crisp raw veggies over any cooked vegetable that she prepared. She was very happy that he had acquired these healthy habits that would stay with him forever. Yet as he turned a teenager, he refused to eat any salad at home. She was intrigued by this sudden change in preference and had come to consult me as he was also putting on weight. After questioning the mother I realized that her son had started eating out often with friends, where he came across salads that were much tastier than those he ate with the regular lemon and salt dressing at home. Elementary, my dear friend, I thought – the salad dressing is the culprit. Salads served in restaurants are likely to have large portions of oily dressing. This rich dressing appeals to most children. When one feasts on foods that are high on sugar or fat, there is a surge of hormones (dopamine and serotonin) that induce a pleasurable feeling. This is why, in spite of knowing that such foods are bad for us, we are drawn to them. It is interesting to note that there are actually very few who will claim to feel rejuvenated after eating such food. Instead, they often feel sluggish and uneasy afterwards. Yet the temporary gratification that we get while eating these fatty, sugary foods overrides the not-so-great after-effects. I recommended some interesting dressings for the boy and he was back to eating salads at home.

Most of us are aware that the regular mayonnaise recipe is not so healthy for two reasons. One, it is loaded with oil and, two, it has raw eggs and carries the risk of Salmonella infections. Do check out a healthy mayonnaise recipe (see *Recipes*) that does not require raw eggs.

Quite evidently, the salad dressing has the ability to make or mar the goodness of a salad. Gone are the days when the salad was made without any hint of fat or oil. In fact, some amount of oil helps to absorb nutrients as the Vitamin A in vegetables is fat soluble. On the other hand, immersing the salad in a rich dressing may seem like the best way to improve the taste, but this would make it a calorie bomb, too. Remember that even when using healthy dressings, it is not a good idea to smother the salad ingredients with them.

Be Salad-Savvy

These guidelines and suggestions will come in handy:

- To preserve the fresh appearance of salads, add the salad dressing just before serving.
- When dining out, you could ask for the dressing on the side so that you could spoon it yourself and control the amount.
- The quality of the oil is important – choose cold-pressed oils whenever possible. Use flavourful oils such as olive, peanut and sesame to complement salads.

- Serve innovatively – in an orange shell, or a scooped-out melon shell. Cutting fruits and vegetables into interesting shapes also makes a difference in the salad's appeal to children.
- When dining out, I know of people who wolf down salad in the hope that it will work wonders for their well being. It is true that salads have great nutritional potential. They can fill your stomach and provide loads of minerals and vitamins. They add colour to the table and usually take little time to prepare. But things can go frightfully wrong if one is not aware of the hazards that salads can pose. For one, when one is not certain about hygiene standards, it would be best to opt for a **cooked salad.** The second danger zone is the kind of hidden ingredients that go into a salad, especially **salad dressings,** which, besides calories, could be loaded with salt and preservatives, too.
- Salads can be served to children as appetizers (fruit salad), accompaniments (tossed green salad), as a main dish (Russian salad), a dessert (Waldorf salad), or as a snack.
- For those who think salads are all about nibbling on leaves, here is the truth – just about anything can go into a salad – fruits, cooked or uncooked vegetables, meat, eggs, nuts, lentils and seeds – to make a complete meal by itself.
- Very often, I am asked if eating raw veggies in a salad is better than cooked veggies in it. It is often thought that raw forms of vegetables are the healthiest. However, in the case of tomatoes, the lycopene content goes

up three times when they are cooked. Cooking also improves the digestibility of certain foods such as sprouts or legumes. That's why it is a good idea to vary the ingredients of the salad and include both raw and cooked vegetables in your child's diet.

- A fusion of flavours and textures makes a salad interesting. Remember to not cut the fruits and vegetables too finely. Very fine chopping causes a greater loss of nutrients. Moreover, the ingredients also lose their identity when very finely chopped.

The season also dictates the kind of salad one would like to consume. Summer meals are incomplete without salads in the same way that soup takes centre stage in a winter meal. A high moisture content of the ingredients makes salads so desirable in the summer. For instance, watermelon and feta cheese is a good combo for the summer months. Carrot and raisin make a good pair for the winter months. Try this one in the winter: Arrange the salad into layers. The bottom layer could be of slightly sautéed green leafy veggies. Over this layer, add a layer of mushrooms or some shredded meat. Add a dressing that your child likes. Mix the layers while eating.

Tips for Salads Making

- Keep salad leaves in a damp cloth or dip the stems in a jug of water. Alternatively, place the greens in a covered container in the refrigerator. Dip the leaves in ice water for a few minutes to make them crisp.
- Avoid chopping herbs and salad leaves very finely. This causes loss of flavour. Many salad leaves can be gently torn or shredded by hand.

HEALTHY SALAD DRESSINGS

FRENCH DRESSING: Mix 2 tbsp vinegar, ½ tsp mustard powder, ½ cup oil, 2 tsp lemon juice, 1 tsp sugar, ½ tsp salt and ½ tsp pepper all together in a bottle and shake well. Shake before use, too, and store in the refrigerator.

HONEY MUSTARD DRESSING: Mix 5 tbsp honey, ½ tsp mustard powder, 1 tsp oil and 4 tsp vinegar.

SESAME GINGER DRESSING: Mix 2 tbsp sesame seeds – toasted and ground, 1 tsp grated ginger, 1 tsp soya sauce, 1 tsp vinegar and 1 tsp sugar.

TOMATO YOGURT DRESSING: Mix 2 tbsp tomato purée, 1 tsp oil and 4 tbsp yogurt.

GARLIC LEMON DRESSING: Mix 2 tsp minced garlic, 2 tbsp lemon juice, ½ tsp oregano powder and ½ tsp onion powder.

OTHER DELICIOUS DRESSINGS

- Jaggery, mint powder, red chilli powder, vegetable oil and lemon juice. Goes well with tomato and cucumber salad.
- Cashew bits blended with olive oil. Add lemon juice and chopped basil leaves. Basil leaves should be chopped just before serving so that they do not turn black.
- Chunky peanut butter mixed with milk.
- Curd dressing can be prepared easily but needs to be done in advance. Tie 100g curd in a muslin cloth and leave for 2 hours for the water to drain. Mix the thick curd into a bowl and whisk till creamy. Add ½ tsp garlic paste, ½ tsp lemon juice, and salt and pepper to taste. Add ½ tsp chopped parsley at the end.

- Always sprinkle fruits with a little lime juice to avoid discoloration. Alternatively, mix the fruits with the dressing immediately to avoid this problem.

- Honey is one of the ingredients I like to use instead of sugar in a salad. Ayurveda has given honey a very prominent place in its scheme of medicinal remedies. Manuka honey from New Zealand has been shown to kill 250 varieties of bacteria, including the deadly MRSA.
- Vinegar is another important ingredient in salad dressings. Traditionally, vinegar has been known for its medicinal properties. Vinegar can be flavoured easily by adding spices or herbs, such as lemongrass. Such flavoured vinegar is called vinaigrette. There are many varieties of vinegar, including *jamun* vinegar, which is very good for digestion, curing skin inflammation, and headache caused by heat.

Combine 3 parts of oil (olive/sesame) with 1 part of vinegar. Add basil paste, sugar, salt and black pepper for a readymade dressing that can be stored in the fridge.

- Make salad dressing more flavourful by grilling garlic cloves over the fire and adding them, sliced, to the oil to be used in the dressing. Let the flavour of garlic seep into the oil and store the leftover oil in the refrigerator.
- Nuts added to salads is one way to get children to eat this vital food. Walnuts and pine nuts as well as sesame seeds go well with many salads.
- The only time to avoid salads is when one is not certain about the washing procedures followed during preparation. As salads usually contain cut fruits and vegetables they should not be left out at room temperature for long periods.

Planning Lunch/Dinner

For the school-going child, the lunchtime meal could be in any of these forms: a school lunch or a packed lunch, or it could be a full meal that the child eats on getting back home from school, or it could be a snack-like item. No matter what the presentation, the guidelines for lunch/dinner are:

- The lunch/dinner should provide for one-third of the child's nutritional requirement. The menu should include foods from at least two or three food families.
- Strike a balance between what the child likes and what is nourishing for him/her. A pizza may be acceptable for lunch as long as it is not the only food item on the menu. Team up the pizza with a healthy beverage and salad. Keep the portion size of the pizza in accordance with the cereal requirement of the child, and you will be dishing out a healthy meal.

Want some Dessert?

In all my meal plans for kids, I do make an allowance for a small portion of dessert 3–4 times a week (usually in the dinner menu when the family eats together). In order to enjoy desserts and yet keep the meal healthy, try the following tips:

- Make a homemade dessert. It will have ingredients that you would like to use.
- Stick to a small portion size and savour the taste. The first few bites are enough to satisfy the craving for sweet food. Bigger is not better in this context.
- Swap unhealthy ingredients for healthier ones. For instance, make fruit purées and add to desserts. This will reduce the need for sugar in the dish.

- Keep desserts for special meals. You don't need to have them every day.
- Cut out processed foods in the diet to make room for dessert on the menu.
- Incorporate healthy foods into desserts. For instance, if you are using a brownie mix to prepare a dessert, add a cup of boiled black-eyed beans (blended to a smooth paste) instead of adding oil and eggs to the mixture. Believe it or not, such swapping not only preserves the taste that children love but also makes the food more nutritious.
- Use apple purée instead of oil in cupcakes. Make applesauce this way: Quarter and core the apple. Put in a food processor and blend for 2 minutes. Add 1 tsp of water if required.
- Swap cream with Greek yogurt for icing a cake and for desserts.
- Swap jam with grated carrots preserved in honey.
- Use your child's favourite fruit to make fruit kebabs – kids love this simple dessert!

Common Deserts

- **Ice Cream:** As a client of mine remarked, any festivity without ice cream sounds quite meaningless. You can go ahead and give your child his or her quota of ice cream after reading this:

If you are looking for ice cream to fulfil your child's calcium needs, make sure to check that ½ cup of the ice cream you choose provides 15 percent of the Daily Value of calcium. Do remember that one portion of ice cream is just ½ a cup of ice cream, which is the size of a tennis ball. Avoid the calorie-loaded variety that has bits of brownies or crumbles or cookies in it. Half a cup of this variety of ice cream can easily be something to the tune of 250 calories. Adding cut fruit to any plain flavour adds nutrients to the creamy dessert while enhancing its satiety value. A 'fresh-fruit-ice-cream' dessert with some nuts makes a great dessert for kids.

- **Chocolates:** Most of us know that dark bitter chocolate is healthy in small portions. Even milk chocolate can be part of a healthy diet provided you remember to add up the calories. A 45g bar provides 234 calories which is one-tenth of the daily need. Sticking to 10–15g (100–150 calories) is not a sin. Dip a fruit in chocolate sauce to provide the taste of chocolate, and increase the portion size and satisfaction levels.

Here is what you can try: Melt ½ cup dark chocolate chips for 30 seconds in the microwave. Stir and check if the chocolate has melted; otherwise, microwave for another few seconds. Dip one portion of walnuts in the melted chocolate and cool. The same procedure could be followed with fruits such as strawberries.

Diet Desserts

Nowadays, plenty of desserts come with the sugar-free label. I was surprised to note that when I asked a gathering of parents what a healthy dessert means to them, almost 90 percent of them said 'sugar-free desserts'. There are a variety of artificial sweeteners that are added to desserts to reduce the calorie intake. A sweeteners such as stevia claims to be natural as it is made from the leaf of the stevia plant.

However, the leaf is processed to remove bitterness so it is not strictly a natural product.

Many 'sugar-free' foods may still have a high fat and calorie content, and can be harmful if consumed in excess.

Honey and Jaggery

It is good to allow children a quota of healthy sweeteners, honey and jaggery being the common examples. Although both honey and sugar provide the same number of calories per gram, there are some benefits of using honey over sugar. It is well known that honey is better than many formulas for night-time cough. Its antibacterial properties and skin- and wound-healing properties are well established. Honey is also used in the treatment of stomach ulcers and *H. pylori* infections. However, it also contains four types of sugar, so it must be used in moderation.

Jaggery, too, has an equal number of beneficial attributes. Being iron-rich is just one of them. Traditionally, an Indian meal was complete only when it ended with a piece of jaggery, which is also a digestive aid. The policosanol in jaggery has cholesterol lowering properties, too!

Finally, when it comes to dessert, remember:

- On most days, limit sugar intake to not more than 4 to 5 tsp of sugar (in all forms). A slice of cake with icing could have as much as 3–4 tsp. A scoop of ice cream would have approximately the same quantity. A cola can/bottle (360ml) would have 32g of sugar, which is 8 tsp.
- Substitute honey and jaggery for refined sugar wherever possible.

[10]

Snacks and In-betweens

These days, I have more and more parents coming to me, quite worried that their children are 'grazing' rather than eating regular meals. Their inability to control this tendency gets them anxious. So let me give the facts clearly to you.

We are programmed to eat every few hours to maintain our energy levels. Therefore, snacking does fit very well into a schedule of healthy eating. This is particularly true for children as they have a smaller stomach and appetite. Naturally, they feel full easily.

I have found that teenaged children are less inclined to eat regular meals for many reasons, one of these being their busy schedules. In such circumstances, too, snacks play an important role in fulfilling nutritional needs. The challenge is to make the right snacks available for children.

Choose snacks that incorporate at least **two** important food groups. Some examples have been cited in the recipes section (see *Recipes*). Also plan the snacks in advance to avoid falling prey to wrong choices because of the lack of time to dish up something quickly.

This is a good time to dismiss the myths around a very popular food used in snacks – potatoes. The truth is that potatoes are a source of carbohydrates and contain no fat. The belief that a potato-free diet will help prevent weight gain is not correct. It is the deep-fried version of potatoes that poses a problem for any healthy diet plan. Baked potato stuffed with cheese/peas or a boiled potato *chaat* with sprouts and chutney can make great, guilt-free snacks without the worry of weight gain or dietary imbalances.

Like potatoes, the banana (again mistakenly considered a fattening food by many, perhaps because of its sweetness), makes a great snack food for kids. Almost perfect in terms of nutrition, the banana comes in a sterile packing, too. The carbs in the banana are of the healthy variety and do not cause a sugar spike like a piece of cake would. The sustained energy release keeps one satiated. The fibre present in this fruit is of the kind that keeps constipation at bay (many people have trouble believing this fact!) There are many ways in which one could combine the humble banana with other foods and make an excellent snack.

Popcorn and movies have been synonymous. Corn by itself is a good snack food. Boiled or roasted corn is yet another great in-between food for children. Corn on the cob spiked with lemon, *chaat* masala or Italian herbs adds to its appeal.

BANANARAMA

Slice the banana into 2–3 portions. Mix peanut butter with enough milk to make it of a batter consistency. Roll the banana sections in this batter, so that they are evenly coated. Roll each banana section in any wholegrain ready-to-eat cereal. Place in the freezer and serve when frozen.

Currently, trendy popcorn versions (strawberry jam popcorn, chocolate crackle popcorn, salted caramel popcorn and so on) are in vogue. Usually, it is the caramel or the sugar or the kind and the amount of fat used that negates the benefit one can derive from corn. The microwave version of popcorn is a cause of concern due to some of the additives, excess salt and oil present in the packet. Moreover, the packaged version of popcorn typically contains trans fats, making it undesirable nutritionally. It is possible to make healthy popcorn in the microwave or in a pressure cooker. Adding nuts and raisins to popcorn helps to make it even better. While on the topic of popcorn, I would like to mention that with the popularity of low-fat foods, the popularity of synthetic butter flavour is also becoming a trend. The chemical diacetyl, which mimics the flavour of butter, has been shown to have some links with Alzheimer's disease, so be aware and beware.

As a nutritionist, I always do my best to swing the balance in favour of unprocessed foods, especially when it comes to snacks. I would encourage a child to have a banana over a piece of cake, even though the calories could be the same in both foods. Now, a word about packaged snacks.

- Today, companies making ***baked snacks*** are laughing all the way to the bank. Diet *namkeens* are flying off the shelves. But the truth is that such snacks may be only a tad better than the fried ones. Such so-called healthier versions of snacks do have reduced fat (sometimes by 50 percent) but to compensate for that, carbohydrates are added. As a result, the calories in the diet snack may be just 10 percent less than those in the fried version. Always compare the two versions in terms of calories and you will be able to see for yourself. The content of sodium, sugar and refined flours is usually higher in the diet versions as a means of compensating for the reduced fat. So be judicious when giving these variants to children.

- There is worldwide data to support a correlation between BMI and the amount of television children watch. This is not only because TV watching makes children inactive but also because they eat more in response to the food promotion they see on it. The presentation of the dish can make a world of a difference in getting children interested in home-cooked food and natural products.
- Advertisements about many of the energy and protein bars touted as healthy snacks can be misleading. Check out their sugar content and you will notice that they are loaded with sugar.

If children are hungry in less than an hour and a half after a meal/snack, then this is not indicative of true hunger. Such hunger arises either out of boredom or because of commonplace emotional issues. At such times, it would be best to channelize the child's attention to other activities, preferably to sports or some other form of exercise. Get them to drink water and then reassess their hunger symptoms.

[11]

BEVERAGES

A recent study cited in the journal *Pediatrics* investigated the cause for abdominal pain in children visiting the emergency room. It emerged that in more than a quarter of the children, the cause for the pain was due to constipation, primarily due to a faulty diet and inadequate fluid intake.

Water

Children today are replacing plain drinking water with all forms of sugary drinks and carbonated drinks. This is a harmful trend that is adversely affecting their health. As a result of this acquired taste for sweetened drinks, children do not want to drink plain water.

COOL IDEAS FOR DRINKING WATER

- Crush some lemongrass leaves into a jug of water and leave it in the refrigerator for half an hour to chill. You can use this water to make other drinks as well.
- Grate the rind of a lemon and add to a jug of water. This lemony taste gets most children to drink enough water. Incidentally, the lemon rind is rich in many antioxidants, too.
- Place some mint leaves in the ice tray and fill it with lukewarm water, and freeze. The ice cubes add extra flavour to plain water!
- Make juice popsicles by freezing juice in ice trays. Add one or two cubes of the juice popsicle to a glass of water to get those kids not in the habit of drinking plain water to get started.

If a child is thirsty, offer water rather than a juice/fruit drink/sherbet. Some amount of juice can be part of the child's daily menu, but it should not be provided as a replacement for water. Do not ask the child: 'What will you drink?' Instead, provide them with the healthy choices you can offer.

We often don't realize it, but it is water that keeps our mind and body functioning well. However, that's not all:

- Water is a universal solvent, which is a wonderful property for many reasons. If your body is hydrated well enough, then you digest your food better, which in turn helps your body to dissolve and absorb the vitamins and minerals that your food contains.
- It keeps your skin healthy.

- It helps to flush out toxins from your body.
- Water also keeps you full, preventing overeating.

A Guide to Water Requirements

1 Although in a healthy child the thirst response could be relied upon to keep him or her well hydrated, it is good if he or she drinks water regularly and not just when thirsty.

2 For adults the 'eight glasses a day' theory has been debunked. It is not valid anymore for prescribing water requirements. For both adults and children, pale yellow urine indicates adequate fluid levels in the body. This is the most reliable indicator with respect to judging adequate hydration.

3 You will be surprised to know that with the loss of just five per cent of body fluids, perceptible symptoms of dehydration appear. Even such a small loss can reduce the capacity for physical and mental effort or activity by 20–30 per cent! Did you know that half the people who complain of fatigue are actually dehydrated?

Safe Water

Getting pure drinking water remains a challenge in the developing world. At present, boiling, ultraviolet rays and chlorination are the popular methods used to make the water potable. A team of researchers looking for a cheaper alternative to purify water have made an interesting discovery. It was observed that dried and powdered cilantro/coriander (*dhania*) when substituted for charcoal in filters, has the ability to remove heavy metals and purify water. The value of the herb has gone up by several notches since then.

You will be surprised to know that all packaged water_is not necessarily safe water. Bottled water may be just ordinary tap water that has been treated, in most cases with ozone, to meet certain quality standards. Packaged and mineral water are different. Although most bottled water is referred to as mineral water, it may not really be so.

- **Mineral water** is water from a spring or well that usually contains 250–500ppm (parts per million) of minerals. Many of these mineral water brands may be high on sodium, which is why children are better off without them.
- **'Enhanced water'** has now become a trend. Water is being marketed with many additives such as vitamins, minerals, herbs, antioxidants and so on.
- **Vitamin water** is bottled water to which certain vitamins have been added. An excess of water-soluble vitamins gets flushed out of the body. The fat soluble vitamins, on the other hand, cannot get absorbed without a fat being present. So this is surely not the best way to give your children vitamins.
- **Tonic water** has a misleading name. It is actually a carbonated drink with added sugar that has been legally classified as a soft drink.
- **Soda water/Sparkling water** has the same ability to hydrate the body as plain water. I recommend sparkling water to relieve symptoms of upset stomach and constipation.

Make it a point to not let your child quench his or her thirst with aerated drinks, coffee or tea. There is clear evidence linking the consumption of aerated drinks to an increased risk of obesity, dental caries and possible behavioural problems in children.

Switching to diet colas or low-calorie drinks in the belief that one is consuming fewer calories does not work. Researchers at Johns Hopkins University, US, have found that those who choose diet drinks are the ones who end up snacking unhealthy. The switch to such drinks is effective only if it is coupled with other healthy dietary interventions.

There are also concerns that diet beverages can actually boost the preference for sweet tastes. There is some indication that too much of these sweeteners could disturb the hunger and satiety hormone operations, leading to a disruption of metabolism.

Two important points:

- Installing water softeners is not a great idea as it increases the sodium content of the water in the process of reducing hardness.
- Store and drink water from stainless-steel or glass utensils. Many plastic containers pose the hazard of BPA, a toxin that leaches into water from plastic bottles, tumblers and cans.

Coconut Water

Coconut Water has been on the Indian coastal menus ever since one can remember. However, it is only recently that it has come into its own in other parts of India, too. Green coconut is now widely available. Thanks to aseptic packing technology, one is able to get the benefit of this drink even when one is not residing close to the sea without losing the natural taste. Coconut water is an isotonic drink, high on potassium, naturally sweet and low in calories. It is a great alternative to carbonated drinks.

Juices

Whenever one thinks of healthy drinks, one invariably visualizes glasses of juice. Juices are loaded with nutrients, are simple to make and easy to consume. Here are some facts about this popular drink.

- Juices are available as either freshly extracted or packaged varieties.
- In the packaged variety, it is crucial to read the nutritional information in terms of the following: if some sugar has been added and if some amount of fibre is available in the juice. Remember, fruit drinks are not juices; they have a fruit juice concentrate along with sugar and water.

Juices made at home are healthier as you can control what goes into it. When making juice at home, one has the opportunity to add back the extracted fibre if one desires.

Some points to be kept in mind when consuming juices:

- Juice can never really be a substitute for whole fruit.
- Most juices have significant calories from sugar. Always add that number to your child's calorie tally for the day.
- Juices may be acceptable if your child does not eat enough fruits and vegetables for some reason (e.g., illness), but you should not choose a juice over a fruit simply because your child prefers it that way.
- Do put the leftover pulp back into the juice and blend it if you do not want to lose vital nutrients of the fruit.

- Consider adding some yogurt/almonds in order to improve the nutritional profile of the juice.
- Juices may interfere with the action of many prescription drugs; for instance, Vitamin-K-rich spinach juice can alter the action of anti-clotting medicines.

The 'juice only diet' is a fad diet that is mistakenly touted as being very healthy. Such extreme and restricted diets slow down the metabolism and are absolutely not recommended for children. There is yet another myth associated with juices. It is believed that the reduced fibre in the juice is important for better absorption of the nutrients that it is providing. It is true that too much fibre can interfere with the absorption of certain nutrients, but the truth is that most people do not get even the minimum requirement of fibre in a day.

Cancer treatment and immunity benefits all come through the consumption of fruits. Juices have no special advantage in cancer treatment or immunity enhancement. So keep in mind that the fruit will always score over its juice!

Tea Truths

Children today are drinking iced tea by the gallon. There are many brands of iced tea powder available, but this drink can be made quite effortlessly at home, too.

I make iced tea (at times, using green tea) at home and my kids prefer it to the taste of the synthetic powders available in the market. Green tea is in vogue and not without reason. The tea leaves are not oxidized and fermented, just dried. They are rich in polyphenols that prevent cancer and heart disease. The catechins present in tea imbue it with amazing antiviral and anti-diarrhoeal properties. However, excessive tea drinking (more than two glasses a day) in teenagers and children may trigger anxiety and insomnia.

Flavoured tea has no additional health benefits, but is popular for its taste appeal. Usually, it takes three minutes to get the flavour from the tea bag. Even though you notice the perfect colour in less than three minutes, the flavour and antioxidants take three minutes to manifest.

Coffee Codes

Coffee is no longer on the 'bad foods' list and cafés are mushrooming in every part of the country. The fear that coffee drinkers are at a greater risk of heart attacks and strokes has been dispelled by many long-term studies.

The good news is that coffee has the ability to rev up the metabolic rate. This implies a better ability to burn off fat and stave off diabetes. Coffee can temporarily increase blood pressure, but there is little evidence that it causes hypertension.

A simple cup of coffee made with the Indian Arabica bean with milk and a little sugar can be a healthy drink. With whipped cream, the calorie value may go over 550 calories.

Children seem to love all variants of coffee: latte, mocha, iced and so on. Depending on the age group of the child, the number of glasses/cups in a week should be monitored – as a general rule, do not exceed 5 to 6 cups a week. It is important to stay within the limit of 1–2 cups per day for older children, too. Overconsumption can lead to symptoms of anxiety, insomnia, restlessness and an upset stomach.

Energy Drinks

A beverage that does great business, especially during the examination season, is the energy drink. In today's stress-ridden world, even the young seem to need extra energy. Guzzling cans of energy drinks to prep themselves for the examinations seems de rigueur. Parents should be careful about offering these drinks to children.

I can understand the attraction for these drinks. The culprit is clever advertising, and we, on our part, ignore the fine-print warnings. Most of the energy packed in these drinks comes from the sugar content, which could be in the form of one or more of the following: glucuronolactone/sucrose/glucose/dextrose and from that time-tested stimulant, caffeine.

The cause for concern is that it is easy to drink several cans of these sweetened beverages, which add up quickly in terms of calories. The other worry is that these drinks contain, besides caffeine and sugar, ingredients like ginseng, guarana, green tea and taurine, an amino acid. Most of these ingredients are stimulants of some sort, and multiple stimulants are often known to interact with undesirable side effects if consumed in large amounts. Symptoms such as an upset stomach, palpitations, jitteriness and nervousness are some of the reactions. Worse, these effects get magnified when energy drinks are consumed on an empty stomach.

Excessive consumption of these highly caffeinated energy drinks could be an indicator of underlying problems that the child may be suffering from, such as depression or anxiety.

The truth is that whenever energy depletion occurs, the body needs to replenish it. The sensible thing to do is to get it from natural foods. After all, one should aim for more than just short-term benefits. Here is what you can do:

- A good night's sleep is a must.
- Enjoyable physical activity in some form counters fatigue to a great extent.
- Yoga is a great stress reducer and energy booster.
- Try and ensure that your kids get enough carbohydrates from fresh fruits, dried fruits like dates, vegetables, cereals, milk and yogurt.
- Don't let them skip meals.
- Dehydration is an important cause of fatigue. So make sure that your kids have enough water, juices, milk shakes, lassi and *nimbu pani*.

It is true that the amount of caffeine one gets from a can of an energy drink is more or less the same as in a cup of coffee. But a cup of coffee is a much safer option than these energy drinks containing multiple stimulants. After all, one knows how the body reacts to 150mg caffeine in a cup of coffee! Just make sure that your child drinks extra water to counter the dehydrating effect of caffeine in the coffee.

Many children believe that a diet drink will help them lose weight. The truth is that drinks with artificial sweeteners (present in diet drinks) disrupt appetite control. It seems that the brain is unable to sense the energy consumption in a reliable manner. As a result, diet drinks may actually result in increased food intake and prove counter-productive. The bottom line is that beverages form an important part of children's diets, but no drink can replace the goodness of water.

[12]

THE TIFFIN BOX

As I go through the daily evening ritual of cleaning out my school-going son's bag – I see books there, a couple of crumpled sheets of paper, some pencils stubs, ink-stained kerchiefs… and then I see the tiffin, half eaten! I am distressed and disappointed. So here goes Mum: Why haven't you eaten your tiffin? Don't you know how I rush in the morning to pack it for you?

Oh Ma! Not again. I was busy/playing/forgot. You also cannot expect me to eat the same food every day!

The last sentence pierces the heart, making one feel like an incompetent parent.

All the earlier gentle nudges come to my mind: *Shubham gets fabulous pizzas, Tarang's tiffin has delicious cutlets and garlic toast… it goes on.*

Oh! Don't worry, Ma – we share our tiffins. I do get to eat a lot of interesting food.

I am sure you, too, are familiar with the parent's daily anguish of trying to pack tasty, nutritious food for school. The demand to have a varied tiffin is also quite a challenge. In fact, it has now become my dream to have my son see me as the Superchef Mum. Somehow, I can't remember my mother facing such daunting competition – we were quite happy with pulao with veggies, or paneer with tomato sauce, or a vegetable sandwich (she, too, was a working parent).

I often wonder: Was it that we were not demanding as kids, or was our exposure to food limited, resulting in fewer demands?

Schooldays are like holidays, especially for working mothers: A glass of milk in the morning with their favourite additive depending on the child's favourite sportsperson, and a tiffin, which could be a sandwich, chips or parathas. But holidays and prep leave can be tiresome for parents who have to plan all meals with the added burden of making them nutritious, filling and tasty all rolled into one. Quite often I am posed the question: What are the healthy snacks that children will readily and happily eat?

I am also aware that junk food has become a way of life, which is why there is an entire section on how to convert the not-so-healthy foods into better choices (See Chapter 14, *Outsmart Junk*).

Let us face it, this is the age of burgers, tacos, burritos, and macaroni and cheese, and they are here to stay. But, with a little bit of tweaking, healthy Indian snacks can be on a child's wish list, too. For instance, a *kathi* roll, a kebab, and egg *bhurji* are simple, snacky, enjoyable dishes that are being overshadowed by their western counterparts.

TIFFIN TIME

Here are a few tasty and nutritious tiffin ideas. (See Recipes)

- Soya nuggets made into cutlets, shallow-fried
- *Besan* toast, shallow-fried, with salsa/chutney
- Boiled corn
- Sweet potato *chaat*
- Sesame spinach toast (base could be of potatoes)
- Black *chana tikki*
- Vegetable idli
- Pasta with nuts and greens
- Wholewheat pancakes layered with honey
- Paneer wrap (mixed flour roti as wrap)
- Peas *poha*
- Carrot–peanut *upma*
- Peanut butter sandwich with shredded lettuce
- Oatmeal cookies/cake

One must involve the kids when planning and executing the tiffin menu. That way they are more likely to eat what they have asked for – made their way!

Variety works well in the tiffin box as children crave change and excitement in their meal at school. For more lunchbox ideas, see the *Recipes* section.

[13]

The Brain-boosting Diet

Come exams and I am flooded with questions regarding good nutrition for children at this stressful time – they are either bingeing as an emotional crutch or are averse to eating because of stress. There are also queries about dietary prescriptions for boosting mental alertness and enhancing memory. My answer is that nutrition is very important, but memory enhancing supplements are still in the realm of research, so they are best avoided.

Let me start with the most vital nutrient – water. These days, students are replacing their requirement for water with sugary drinks, energy drinks, tea and coffee. Such replacements not only result in unwanted calories, caffeine and other stimulants being imbibed but also lead to inadequate hydration. It has been observed that the common symptom of fatigue amongst students is often linked to poor water intake.

The other crucial factor is the energy balance of the body. Blood sugar levels can affect energy levels and the ability to think lucidly. Refined carbohydrates raise blood sugar levels rapidly. However, such a sudden spike in blood sugar levels is not at all desirable. Moreover, such spikes are always followed by a slump in the sugar level, leaving one tired and fatigued. Getting a steady source of energy is crucial and this can be achieved if one eats those carbohydrates that have adequate fibre and thus release energy slowly over time. These are derived from fruits, vegetables, beans, lentils and whole grains.

Protein-rich foods such as eggs, fish and poultry are known to boost alertness. Let me explain how. Proteins, when digested, break down into amino acids, one of which is tyrosine. This tyrosine is documented as being able to increase the production of neuro-transmitters, which in turn enhance alertness and energy levels. By eating protein-rich foods, the level of tyrosine increases. But this happens only when the protein is eaten alone. If the protein is combined with carbohydrates, this benefit is somewhat curtailed.

This is why eggs are a great choice on the morning of exams. In addition to tyrosine, they are rich in choline, too. Choline is a vitamin of the B-complex group that is a precursor of the brain neuro-transmitter acetylcholine, which is linked to memory. Experiments have shown that when drugs were administered to block choline, people have failed memory tests.

Vegetarians, take heart. There are many protein foods for you, too, on the brain-boosting list – milk, tofu, cheese, peanuts, walnuts, peas and legumes do this job as well.

Fats are important for nerve health. The ideal choice for fat would be one with an adequate ratio of omega-3 fatty acids. To test the importance of nutrients for brain health, a study was conducted on about 800 children in Australia, who were supplemented with omega-3 fatty acids and micronutrients (iron, zinc, folate and Vitamins A, B_6, B_{12} and C) in a drink mix. These students reported higher scores on tests that measured verbal intelligence, learning and memory after 6 and 12 months. Oils derived from mustard seeds, canola, soya bean or sesame seeds would be a good choice. Children can munch on walnuts, sunflower and watermelon seeds. These can be added to salads and smoothies as well. Cut down on packaged and fried foods.

Poor dietary habits in children lead to low iron-status, causing anaemia. The link between low haemoglobin levels and a reduced ability to concentrate is well known. That is why you need to give particular attention to the adequacy of iron, folic acid and Vitamin B_{12} in your child's diet. Foods rich in iron are almonds, eggs, chickpeas, peanuts, soya, dates, jaggery and raisins. The B_{12} sources are mostly of animal origin; some vegetarian sources are fermented foods and yeast. The folate-rich foods are green leafy vegetables, oranges, mushrooms and green beans.

Zinc and magnesium found in meats and seeds are antioxidants necessary for cognitive processes and memory.

The Mind-Body Connect

Memory or recall is a complex process and no single food can take care of all that goes into it. Besides food, the role of exercise in improving blood circulation is very crucial. Do make sure that your child eats well and gets time to exercise, too, preferably outdoors. Children who are physically active in any form (who run, jump, hop, chase, kick a ball) show the greatest improvement in their cognitive scores. Therefore, time devoted to physical fitness will also improve thinking and learning!

The importance of sleep in memory and recall is often overlooked. One of the main purposes of sleep is to allow our brain to process the information one has learnt during the day. If one does not sleep enough, this process of learning will be impaired. The leading expert on sleep, Prof. Russell Foster, professor of circadian neuroscience at Brasenose College at the University of Oxford, UK, advocates eight hours of sleep for mental as well as physical well being. If your child is sleepy throughout the day besides the afternoon dip, which is normal, you should be worried. The following measures will be useful for children who need help in this area:

- Limit the exposure to light at night before bedtime. Turn off the TV, computer screens and mobiles. The blue light emitted from the screens suppresses the hormone that controls sleep-wake cycles.
- Limit intake of caffeine-containing drinks late in the evening. This includes aerated drinks and energy drinks.
- Change the attitude towards sleep. Sleep is not an impediment to success, nor is it an indulgence. The lack of it poses serious problems. Many mental health problems are preceded by sleep-cycle disruption.
- There is enough evidence that *tulsi* leaves help the body fight fatigue, increase stamina and reduce stress. Just the answer for a child with examination fever! It

also improves different facets of memory: working, reference and spatial. Look for the dark variety of *tulsi* (Krishna *tulsi*) to get the benefit of a higher antioxidant content. If your child cannot eat the leaves, add them to pesto sauce (basil, garlic, nuts and cheese). Or add

IMMUNITY BOOSTERS

Building immunity can keep sickness away. Here are a few suggestions you can use to build up your child's immunity, especially during exam time:

1. Give them plenty of yogurt. It contains beneficial bacteria that help boost immunity, ward off cold and cough, and prevent diarrhoea.
2. It is now known that taking raw garlic at the onset of a cold can effectively snuff out the cold.
3. Fruits and veggies with Vitamin A and C, such as oranges, guavas, *amla* and green leafy vegetables, are especially important. Choose vegetables with darker colours as they are richer in beneficial compounds.
4. Omega-3 fatty acids help boost immunity and reduce inflammations. Fish is a good source of omega-3 fats, and for the vegetarians the sources are green leafy vegetables, walnuts, legumes and flaxseeds. I like to make mustard paste by grinding mustard seeds rich in omega-3 fats with some vinegar, and use this for sandwiches and with breads.
5. Zinc is found in the seeds of pumpkin, watermelon, soya and other beans, and yeast. Meat and poultry are sources of zinc for non-vegetarians. Zinc helps prime the immune system and keeps infections at bay.
6. Herbal teas can be part of the beverage allowance. Adding *tulsi*, black pepper, ginger and honey helps work against cough, cold and fever and prevent their onslaught, too.

the crushed leaves to lassi or tea. Did you know that it takes all of 10 fresh leaves of the *tulsi* plant every day for your child to benefit from its amazing properties?

- Antioxidant-rich foods are good for the brain. Fruits and vegetables are loaded with antioxidant power. Prunes, raisins, spinach, plum, beetroot, oranges, red grapes, red capsicum, cherries, onions, corn and brinjal score high on antioxidant power and should be included in the menu in any form that the child enjoys. Turmeric or *haldi* is another powerful antioxidant and quite fortunately our kids eat it regularly. If they are not doing so, add some turmeric to mustard paste in their sandwiches.

Brain-boosting Strategies

Make sure you follow these guidelines for your child, especially during exams.

1 Get the child to drink plenty of fluids – water, barley water, lemonade, cocoa drinks, soups, smoothies and some of the drinks suggested under 'Beverages' in the *Recipes* section.

2 Offer your child small meals at intervals of 2–3 hours. You will find many suitable food items to dish up in the *Recipes* section.

3 The importance of appropriate snacks in such a diet is vital: try popcorn, foxnuts (*makhana*), sweet potato *chaat* and yogurt.

4 Ensure that your child consumes five portions of fruits and vegetables every day. These are powerful brain foods.

5 Limit caffeine by restricting energy drinks, coffee and colas as their increased intake could lead to dehydration and irritability.

6 Many memory-enhancing supplements contain phosphatidylserine (a chemical required for cell function and signalling). This is a naturally occurring nutrient in common foods such as rice, soya, green leafy vegetables and cabbage. A well balanced diet will provide this nutrient.

Finally, one could reinforce the exam diet with that magical spoonful of '*dahi-cheeni*' for good luck before the child leaves home for the exam. This has been an age-old tradition in many parts of India. I had always wondered as a child why it was so and now I have the answer. The bugs in the yogurt are friends, indeed. Eating yogurt is one way to get the quota of Vitamin B_{12}, so crucial for memory!

The truth really is that there is no one 'magic food' guaranteed to help boost mental performance. Long-term benefit can only be derived through eating well balanced meals.

THE DARK SIDE: WHAT NOT TO EAT

- **Processed and packaged items such as chips, *namkeens***
- **Foods that spike blood glucose levels such as instant noodles, sugar-laden cakes, doughnuts**
- **Sugary drinks, fruit juices with added sugar, fruit drinks**
- **Omega-6 fats in large amounts (sunflower/corn/safflower oil)**
- **Drinks containing caffeine in excess**

SECTION 5

DEALING WITH DIETARY PROBLEMS

[14]

OUTSMART JUNK

If you have watched the documentary *Supersize Me*, you would know that American filmmaker Morgan Spurlock, in just four weeks of being on a steady junk-food diet, put his life in danger. The relationship between dietary factors and disease is very strong. There are more than 80,000 dietary factors such as vitamins, minerals, antioxidants and pigments that have been studied and found to have an impact on health and disease.

What really is junk food? Any food with poor nutritional worth (low in minerals, vitamins and other essential nutrients, and high on harmful ingredients) is termed junk food. Unhealthy junk food is popular as it is made appetizing by the use of additives, flavour enhancers, high sugar and lots of fat. The tastiness of such foods promotes overeating.

There is no denying that processed food and junk food are here to stay. There is little point in not allowing the child to eat chips. If one were to strictly ban such a food, it would only increase its appeal to the child. Instead, we should help children to limit its consumption and be selective about it.

For instance, I always recommend that junk food should be *plated* (you take out a portion of the food and place it on the child's plate instead of letting him or her dig into large packets of the food). I have also attempted to turn many of the not-so-healthy foods (that children seem to love) into healthier options without compromising the taste (see box 'From Junk to Joy' later in this chapter).

I had always wondered if it was the attention-grabbing names coined for some of the junk foods available that add to their appeal. This belief of mine has been confirmed by a study with preschoolers conducted by Brian Wansink and others of Cornell University, US, that confirms that 'cool' names given to vegetables can get children to eat and like them. I know many boys in the age group of 3–5 years who like spinach because Popeye eats it. Girls in the same age group eat more greens because their favourite story character with long, shiny hair eats beans, broccoli and the like regularly. Dear parents, try inventing interesting names for nutritious dishes and get your child to eat more of the good stuff. 'Tasty Treetops' (broccoli), 'Power-Punch' (spinach), '20/20 Vision' (carrots) and 'Silly Dilly Green Beans' (beans) are some names that have been tried with positive results. Adopt this easy and time-tested way to counter the junk-food obsession! Surprisingly, the same study cited above showed that even adults responded positively to cleverly named food items.

There is no denying that salt, sugar and fat combos are the magic ingredients that make junk food so irresistible. The food industry has mastered the art of balancing these three ingredients in such a way that the taste buds get titillated, making you crave for more. Often, the melt-in-the-mouth feeling fools the brain into believing that very few calories are being consumed. This could lead to passive overeating and a host of attendant problems.

But do not lose heart – it is possible to make children's all-time favourite dishes appetizing as well as more body-friendly by reducing calories and improving the nutrient worth. This is the most appropriate way forward.

Firstly, look into the method of cooking employed, which can make or mar the nutritional worth of the food item. The same food – depending on how it is cooked and served – becomes healthy or unhealthy. This table will give you some idea about this:

Food Group	Healthy	Not-So-Healthy	Unhealthy
Fruit	Fresh (any) with edible peel	Juiced	Juice with added sugar
Rice	Brown rice, parboiled	Polished milled	Polished milled rice, fried
Bread	Wholegrain	Refined flour	Cakes, croissants with cream
Noodles	Steamed noodles with veggies	Instant noodles with no veggies	Deep-fried crispy noodles
Indian bread	*Methi/palak* roti	*Maida* roti/ naan	*Kachori*, puri, butter naan

Food Group	Healthy	Not-So-Healthy	Unhealthy
Potatoes	Baked/ boiled	Shallow-fried	French fries, other deep-fried forms
Veggies	Steamed, stir-fried, raw	Overcooked	Deep-fried
Salad	Fresh	Cut and stored over long period	With oily/creamy dressing
Fish	Steamed, grilled	Creamy gravies, breaded	Breaded and deep-fried
Sauce/ gravy	Tomato, mint, basil, mustard	With excess oil/butter	Cream-based
Meats	Stewed, pressure-cooked, roasted	Rich gravies, preserved with salt and breaded	Creamy gravy, fried, preserved with salt
Milk	Low-fat	With added sugar	*Khoya*, cream, and high-fat milk with sugar

FROM JUNK TO JOY

Transform your children's favourite food into a healthy alternative with just a simple trick or two.

PIZZA: Make the base at home with wholegrain flours and nuts. Go for extra tomato sauce and veggies. When ordering a pizza, always order a thin-crust one that is made with whole grain. If the pizza base seems greasy, blot the grease on a paper towel before serving.

BURGER: Make the patty with *rajma*/*chana*/sprouts/chickpeas. Instead of mayonnaise, use a yogurt dressing and lots of lettuce leaves/any other readily available veggies. When making meat patties, add vegetable

purée/finely chopped veggies into the patty. Cook the patty on a skillet with minimum oil, or bake in the oven with a little oil glazing.

PASTA: A tomato or bean paste would be ideal for pasta. Add veggies: onions, broccoli, capsicum, tomatoes, corn or mushrooms, or shredded meat.

FRENCH FRIES: Try grilled garlic potato wedges (see 'One Potato Two potato' in *Recipes*) instead. Potatoes when not fried are actually quite healthy. Combine potatoes with a bean salad for optimum nutrition.

BREAD: Substitute plain butter with peanut butter/almond butter. Two tbsp of the nut-butter will provide as much protein as 30g lean meat. Use peanut butter instead of some of the starchy foods that go into sandwiches. Contrary to the widely held belief, nuts taken in moderation can reduce bad cholesterol and lower triglycerides. Add mushrooms, sprouts, lettuce and cucumber pickled in vinegar to sandwiches.

SAUCES: Use healthy sauces such as mustard sauce, which contains 3 per cent of the iron requirement in just a couple of teaspoons. Alternatively, fresh salsa made with tomatoes, garlic and green chillies is also great for kids.

Dining out is becoming a regular feature of our lives. However, dining out with young kids can be quite demanding as one tries to balance taste and nutrients. To overcome this problem, even if the restaurant has a kids' menu, do not go for it. The kids' menu usually has a higher fat content combined with a lower quantity of healthy nutrients.

Here are a few tips for a healthier dining experience you can share with your child:

Tandoori Meal: This kind of meal is healthier than one with deep-fried foods, as long as you avoid the burnt portions of the food. The ideal choices for tikkas are fish or tofu, and veggies.

One could request the chef to skip the basting with oil, usually done after the food comes out of the tandoor. Ask for a liberal coating of marinades made from curd and spices. As far as the roti goes, the plain tandoori or *missi* roti would be better than the naan, *roomali* roti or the *sheermal*. Tandoori sweet potato, beetroot, mushrooms or potatoes are great starters!

Italian Meal: Go for the wholewheat-grain pasta and be mindful about the sauces. Tomato sauce and marinara sauce (tomato-onion-garlic) are the healthiest and should be preferred over the Alfredo or the carbonara. The healthier Italian salad dressings are those with balsamic vinegar, basil, pepper, lemon juice and olive oil. Go for those! Make sure that the pasta and vegetables are in equal proportions, and you are on the right track.

Chinese/Japanese Meal: Avoid the popular starters and go for the steamed dumplings. Good choices amongst Chinese soups are sweet corn, clear soups and bean-curd soup. Ask the chef to cut down on ajinomoto wherever possible. Steamed rice/brown rice is better than Schezwan rice. When choosing noodles, try buckwheat noodles or bean thread noodles. For meat lovers, the steamed meats with veggies and tofu are a smart choice. Choose the right sauces, such as Hunan and oyster, and give the deep-fried dishes a miss.

Thai Meal: The raw papaya salad is a great choice to start a Thai meal. Raw vegetables as an accompaniment would be a good idea as many of the Thai dishes tend to be spicy. Dishes that are labelled 'crispy' or 'crunchy' indicate that they are deep-fried, so skip them.

With some portion control, substitution and a little innovation it is possible to rework the food that children love into acceptable foods from the nutritional standpoint.

[15]

Weighty Issues and More

Kids, I will be late from work. Could you guys just order a pizza?' Today, this is the typical scenario in homes with working parents. Or else, a modified system in some homes is that the help serves the child food that he/she mindlessly eats while watching TV.

The growing-up years are a difficult time for both parents and children. Both over- and undernourishment leads to complications and harm. Childhood obesity is on the rise. The implications of obesity are not limited to health issues such as diabetes, hypertension and liver disease but also to psychological issues including poor self-image and depression. Overweight children commonly become victims of callous teasing, which isolates them. Such children tend to overeat to compensate for the hurt, leading to a vicious weight-gaining cycle. With this in mind, it makes sense to be careful about keeping weight off right from early childhood by following simple diet rules. Worldwide, 200 million schoolchildren are estimated to be overweight. Did you know that children as young as six months old can become overweight? We sure are in some danger as a study by A. Malhotra, published in the *Journal of Obesity and Metabolic Research*, found that 24 per cent of 8–18 year olds in India are overweight and/or obese. Without doubt, prevention needs to begin in the early years.

Fighting food cravings and following fad diets for long are certainly not recommended. In fact, yo-yoing weight is a problem with those who are chronically on some diet or the other, and this is not good from the nutritional point of view. Most overweight people blame weight on genes, but the fact is that there are very few naturally thin people. Most have to work at it! Keeping thin also has a cultural dimension – look at the French, Japanese and Mediterranean people! Their food practices lead to a majority of them being healthier than the rest of the world population.

At the other extreme are kids whom no amount of cajoling can persuade to eat enough. The desire of teenage girls to be like size-zero heroines is so strong that they would rather not eat! Such practices lead to health problems arising from the lack of certain nutrients, a fact that is not emphasized enough. But getting such young people to eat healthy and stay off fad diets is very challenging.

Managing weight should never be an ongoing fight with oneself, for food and exercise were meant to be enjoyable parts of the child's daily life. Maintaining fitness should be a breeze. By the simple arithmetic of the elementary school level: all your child needs to do is to burn more calories than he or she consumes! The number one secret to maintaining a healthy weight is really to control portion size.

I was witness to an interesting experience regarding this. A friend and I went for lunch on a beautiful February afternoon. The hostess was known for her cooking skills. The lunch table was beautifully laid out. The silver *thaalis* sparkled. There were six *katoris* on each plate. My friend, who is rather fond of food, was dreaming of the pleasurable experience about to unfold. But her poor stomach ached for more. The size of the *katoris* was so small that the contents of six *katoris* could not match one of hers. To top it, the chapattis were miniature versions of her usual ones at home. She was embarrassed to ask for more. The variance in portion size in different homes could not have been clearer. A *bowl* means different sizes to different people. Similarly, the size and the thickness of chapattis and parathas vary from home to home. Such variations in portion sizes can have a huge impact on the total calories. In this context, remember, small is beautiful!

The food industry is also making efforts to follow this principle. A well-known US-based chocolate company has decided to restrict the calorie count of its chocolate bars so that it does not exceed 250 calories. Downsizing is one way.

Inappropriate food substitution: If there is no mental picture of how much a certain quantity is, then one can be fooled by it quite easily. For instance, when trying out a recipe, 6oz of butter may not seem like a big amount, but it is nearly as much as two 100g packs of butter! A standard *katori* or cup holds approximately 240ml of food. A standard teaspoon holds 5ml and a tablespoon, 15ml.

Disguised calories: Diet foods can be deceptive. Often, the fat content is reduced and the low-fat version is touted for its health benefits. On close inspection, you would notice that the health food that claims to be low in fat is actually high on sugar/fructose corn syrup/salt or a combination of these taste enhancers. Substituting natural foods with packaged 'healthy' foods is yet another faulty trend these days. When a food is marketed as diet food, quite naturally we tend to allow our kids liberal quantities. Many so-called diet foods may be low in fat but high on sugar content (high fructose corn syrup), which keeps the calorie count identical. Do make sure to check labels of 'diet' foods!

Speed eating is a faulty habit that can fool the body into thinking that it is not yet full. Speed eating triples the risk of developing weight problems! It takes the stomach 20 minutes to register sensations of fullness. This clearly means that if one were to polish off a meal in 10 minutes, the activation of control mechanisms would not take place and, hence, one is very likely to overeat.

Frequency of eating: These days many nutritionists recommend the 'eat every 2 hours' approach to losing weight. This very popular method, which I call 'grazing' (small, frequent meals), should not be standard advice for losing weight. In my practice, I find that this approach often leads to mindless eating, with the inclusion of unhealthy packaged snacks. Advice on the frequency of meals should be provided with caution, after an individual assessment of the personality and the existing environment of the individual.

Parents are often witness to weight-loss programmes that young people undertake. Here are some tips you could share with them so that they stay in the safe zone:

Here is a query that I received from a teenager regarding the eating schedule to be followed when one is trying to lose weight.

Q. I am a 17-year- old girl. I weigh 67kg and my height is 5'4". I exercise regularly. I have heard that eating 5-6 meals a day helps one to lose weight. Is it true? If yes, please explain how it helps.

Here is my response:

Dear Reader,

It is true that following a six-meal (frequent) pattern has been touted as a method to rev up the metabolism, allowing one to lose weight. However, there is no strong evidence to support this very popular notion. It is important to recognize that each one of us has unique nutritional needs. It is true that eating every three hours may work to control appetite for some people. However, the very same pattern may play havoc for someone else who does not have access to the right foods for frequent consumption. Some people also find it difficult to stop eating once they get started. In the case of such individuals, it is better to stick to the regular three-meal pattern.

The important points to remember are that an irregular eating pattern and skipping meals definitely spell trouble for everyone. Intake of food at regular intervals sends signals to the body that there is no need to store energy/calories as there is enough available from time to time. This prevents unnecessary weight gain.

> **For achieving weight loss, it is important to recognize true hunger signals and eat only then. If the time gap seems to be short, it would be best to wait for 20 minutes and check again if you are still hungry. If one gets ravenously hungry, the possibility that it will be followed by overeating becomes great.**
>
> **Meal planning for achieving weight loss should ideally be based on individual lifestyle assessment.**

Top Tips

- It is not advisable to starve, but eating up to the point where one feels satiated is good.
- Eating at intervals of 3–4 hours works well for most people.
- The golden rule is to consistently eat around the same time each day. The amount of food may vary, based on feelings of hunger–appetite.
- Switching off the TV and phones during meals is also a healthy habit.
- Ensure a gap of at least an hour and a half before the child goes to bed after dinner. The good old habit of eating dinner early was not a bad idea at all.
- Bedtime snacking may lead to weight gain, too.
- Slashing too many calories is another mistake that dieters tend to make. Excessive restriction of calories can be a big mistake.

It is not a good idea to go below 1,000–1,200 calories unless advised for medical reasons. Crash diets reduce the calorie-burning ability of the body and thus become counterproductive in the long run. A contestant who participated in *The Biggest*

Loser show shared that the extreme dieting and exercise regimen on the show (she lost 118 pounds) led to hair fall because of vitamin deficiency. She also felt unhealthy. Teenagers who watch shows like that should hopefully learn that there is much more to lose than just weight when following these crash diets.

Chew on This

Reducing liquid calories (sweetened beverages like soda, fruit juice or iced tea) when trying to cut calories is more effective than cutting down intake of any solid food. Therefore, the first things to go off the list should be these liquid offenders.

Chewing makes it easier to eat less and provides feeling of satiety, too. Ayurveda prescribes that each morsel should be chewed 32 times – once for each tooth. Such an exercise prevents overeating as the stomach gets ample time to send a signal to the brain about its being full (before one has already overeaten). Children should be taught early on that food needs to be chewed and not gulped down hurriedly.

Imagine chewing on one small-sized apple, which would typically have 100 to 150 calories versus having a small scoop of dessert made with cream and thickened milk of the same calorie content. The process of chewing and eating some fibre will fill you up much better than any sugary, creamy dessert, even though the calories may be equal in both.

This is why one should prefer a mango/banana over a dessert. It may have the same number of calories, but the dessert is unlikely to have the fibre and the micronutrients that the fruit does!

The Truth about Calories

Calorie is a measure of the energy derived from a food source. However, not all calories are alike in terms of quality. The calories that you derive from fruits and vegetables will always be superior to the calories derived from fast food and sodas, even though the number of calories may be the same in both foods. In the same vein, 50 pistachio nuts may have the same calories as 15 potato chips, but the way in which these calories are metabolised in the body is not the same. It makes sense to choose the health-promoting calories that rev up your metabolism and suppress the 'bad genes' that could promote disease. To get the 'full' feeling, do the following:

- Include water-loaded foods – such as cucumbers and watermelons – as you get water along with the beneficial nutrients that keep you gratified for a longer time.
- Eat similar meals. Repetition of the same foods frequently day after day tends to make one feel fuller and satisfied, and prevents overeating.
- Add herbs and spices in plenty: cinnamon, cardamom, saffron, basil and mint, all help.

WAYS TO CURB CRAVINGS

CHEWING GUM: Suppresses hunger and craving for snacks.

STAY AWAY FROM FOOD ODOURS: As an example, smelling non-food odours such as floral scents could help to reduce cravings fro chocolate.

DISTRACT THE MIND: Diversion from food thoughts helps to reduce the craving for food. Better still, get your child to play a game, listen to music or get involved in his/her favourite activity.

A SUCCESSFUL STORY

The Government of Singapore has taken up the fight against obesity on a serious footing. Their target is the wired generation that prefers the indoors to the outdoors, and on whose staple diet are the television, computer and other gizmos. The scene of action is the school itself.

Primary school children are monitored for height, weight and BMI. The overweight kids are made to join clubs where they run, skip, dribble and perform other exercises over and above the regular ones, until they lose weight.

Joining the 'health club' is compulsory for the overweight kids. This has made the children very conscious of their BMI scores! On the home front, parents are advised on how to cook in a healthier fashion. Adopting such an approach in Singapore has been a success whereas the rest of the world is still grappling with the problem of obesity. The little nation realized that to tackle progressively rising health-care costs, it needs to catch them young.

All fad diets have a common element: a short shelf life. If one is constantly controlling what one eats, is it a surprise when one rebels after a while? This is the reason that the Atkins, South Beach and Zone diets have had to make way for the newer set of fads. After all, it is almost impossible to stay on deprivation or monotonous diets beyond a point. The compromise one makes on taste when one is on a 'bizarre' diet is another reason for its failure in the long run. For example, if one is made to forgo all sweet, glazed and fried foods in favour of the bland and boiled kind, it becomes difficult to persevere for long. In the long run, such diets are harmful as well.

THIN KIDS ALSO NEED TO EAT HEALTHY

The importance of inculcating healthy eating habits is crucial for all children, even those who may be thin despite an unhealthy diet. During the growing-up phase, children are able to burn calories due to their high metabolism and activity levels. However, the taste for salty and sugary food, once formed, continues well into adult life. The result is that these thin kids grow into obese adults when their metabolism slows down.

Food Allergies, Intolerance and Deficiencies

Many children may suffer from food allergies, food intolerance or nutrient deficiencies, and it is important to alter the diet of the child accordingly. The modification required could be to exclude or enhance certain foods or nutrients, or to change the consistency or texture of foods. Food sensitivity and food allergy are synonymous terms. Intolerance to a food is the inability to consume normal amounts of a food for reasons not connected with the immune system (as is the case with allergies). Food intolerance is caused by certain other conditions such as low digestive enzymes or juices.

- **Iron Deficiency Anaemia:** Fatigue and loss of energy are the telltale signs of this common deficiency among children. Cranky and irritable behaviour could be linked to this deficiency. This nutrient also has an impact on the development of children, in a somewhat permanent fashion. Iron-deficient children perform less well on psychomotor testing than those free from this deficiency. Make sure to include good sources of iron in the child's diet: meats, eggs, dark green leafy vegetables, peas, beans, lentils, nuts, and dried fruits such as figs and raisins. Also keep in mind that Vitamin C increases the absorption of iron by almost 2 to 3 times the usual. For instance, peas in tomato purée will lead to better absorption of the iron in the peas as opposed to eating peas exclusively. Also, cooking in cast-iron utensils may not be the trendiest way to cook, but it certainly helps in getting rid of anaemia.

- **Food Allergies:** Allergies usually develop during infancy and childhood, and even more so if there is a family history of the same. A child could be allergic to any food, but the most common allergens are milk, eggs, peanuts, soya, wheat, tree nuts (walnuts, cashews), fish and shellfish. This is why *The American Academy of Paediatrics* offers the following advice for those infants who are at risk (where both parents are diagnosed with allergies):
  - Not to introduce solid food in the infant's diet before the child is a year old.
  - Dairy products including animal milk should be introduced only after the child is a year old.
  - Introduce eggs in the diet only after age two.
  - Serve peanuts, other nuts and fish only after the child is three years old.

The food allergy reaction varies: It could be in the form of a rash/hives on the skin or abdominal pain/vomiting/diarrhoea. It could also manifest as sneezing/wheezing, difficulty in breathing or as light-headedness or fainting. A skin test and a blood test (RAST) could confirm the diagnosis. The reassuring part is that most kids with food allergies outgrow them. Your doctor may recommend a 'food challenge' to assess the status. Once diagnosed, the only treatment is to avoid the allergens by not eating the foods that contain them. No medication is known to cure food allergies.

Gluten allergy/sensitivity is one such trouble that usually begins in childhood. Once the diagnosis is confirmed, the special diet free from gluten (the protein found in wheat, rye and barley) is the only way to stay healthy and avoid complications. It is easy to substitute wheat with a variety of cereals (such as millets like ragi, jowar and bajra), but the difficult part is avoiding wheat in packaged, processed food. Read food labels (ingredients) carefully to watch out for starch, thickeners, fillers and malt.

SECTION 6
THE WAY FORWARD

[16]

SUPERFOODS

In recent times, there has been much coverage of foods that are supposed to be extraordinarily rich in one particular nutrient. Colourful pictures of golden kiwi, blueberries and their ilk are in preponderance. The irony is that we seem to have discovered superfoods only after they caught on in the west. Our own traditions – so rich and valuable since time immemorial – have been largely ignored or even forgotten. For instance, Ayurveda has recognized and incorporated many indigenous superfoods to make medicines and health products. The Ayurvedic tradition states categorically that every plant has health-related value for our bodies. We have a large assortment of our very own superfoods.

So what should be called a superfood? In the popular imagination, any food item ranging from a vitamin to one having a steroidal base, or even foods such as coffee and energy drinks qualify as superfoods. However, in the true and even technical sense, a superfood is a food that has the ability to provide health benefits beyond the nutrients present in it, through the presence of phytonutrients.

The fashion statement today is to enumerate how many superfoods one has managed to include in the family's diet. This label of a superfood keeps shifting from one food to the another. It started with broccoli and blueberries, and moved to flaxseeds and quinoa. The latest on the list are chia seeds, goji berries and yuzu juice. The downside of such publicity is that people tend to spend a lot for nutrients that can be derived just as well from indigenous and lesser known products.

In fact, the Indian gooseberry (*amla*) is as valuable and beneficial, if not more, as the much touted and exquisite blueberries and that, too, at less than a quarter of the price! *Amla* has 20 times more Vitamin C than oranges and, quite surprisingly, this is retained well even when the fruit is dried. *Amla* is also a great immunity booster as well as an anti-ageing agent. It has the ability to enhance the immune response of the body and prevent the onset of infections, which is why *amla* has been incorporated in many Ayurvedic preparations. Kids may not like the fresh form of the fruit as it is slightly bitter, but several preparations made from this food can add nutritive worth to your child's diet (see under the Beverages category in *Recipes*).

Among fruits, the humble guava deserves to be taken note of. It is a human trait not to attribute much worth to anything that does not cost an arm and a leg. A recent study conducted at the prestigious National Institute of Nutrition, Hyderabad, clearly proves how wrong we can be. Among all the fruits studied (including pomegranates, oranges and so on), the antioxidant content of guava stands way above the rest (500mg per 100g of fruit as opposed to 300 mg per 100g in oranges). This is quite a revelation as most of us tend to believe that the more expensive fruits, such as pomegranate and grapes, have a higher antioxidant content.

Phalsa, *jamun* and *ber* are the Indian berries with an unusually high content of phytosterols and phenolic compounds that impart significant health benefits. These berries are India's answer to the much acclaimed goji and acai berries. *Jamun*, the Indian blackberry, is known for its ability to reduce blood sugars and for its digestive properties. *Jamun* also has a high resveratrol content, which works to protect the heart from coronary artery disease. *Phalsa*, available during the midsummer heat, is acclaimed as a cooling agent and a digestive. The *karaunda* is another fruit rich in pectin, iron, Vitamin C and the purple pigment. It takes well to making many kinds of chutneys, which are not only tasty but also loaded with nutritional worth. Coconut pulp provides us good fats similar to those found in avocados. In fact, avocados provide the same nutrients as cooked spinach does with respect to cataract prevention.

The food that is now being recognized as a powerful food is cow's ghee (clarified butter). In fact, it is becoming akin to olive oil in status. A large number of Ayurvedic formulations use cow's ghee as an important ingredient. Cow's ghee is a rich source of CLA (conjugated linoleic acid), which is a very special fatty substance available from dairy sources.

CLA is formed by the action of intestinal bacteria in the cow's gut. CLA supplements are becoming popular as they help in reducing body fat (by increasing fat oxidation and reducing triglyceride uptake), besides offering a host of other benefits. Scientists are looking at this special fat as a weapon against breast cancer, too. However, this certainly does not imply that cow's ghee can be consumed without any restrictions on quantity.

Although coconut oil was at one time frowned upon by the medical fraternity, it has always been greatly cherished in the Indian tradition for its therapeutic properties. The antibacterial and antiviral properties of coconut oil have recently been established with the help of scientific studies.

FACTS ABOUT COCONUT OIL

It is true that the fat in coconut oil is mainly of the saturated variety, which is why it fell out of favour during the 'anti-saturated-fat' drive. What is being realized now that not all saturated fat is alike. The saturated fat that comes from a vegetable source does not cause heart disease and cholesterol problems. The problems occur when the coconut oil is hydrogenated and, as a result, contains trans fats. If coconut oil is used in conjunction with other healthy fats, there are many benefits that accrue from it. The antimicrobial lipid present in it (monolaurin) protects against viruses and bacteria. As in all other oils, go for virgin coconut oil.

Turmeric (*haldi*) is an established star food as it has anti-inflammatory and anti-cancer properties. In the Indian tradition, *haldi* is an integral part of our food as well as cosmetics. The benefits of turmeric increase several fold if 3 parts of turmeric are mixed with 1 part of black pepper. Put this mixture in a salt shaker and use it to rev up your child's immunity. This works as a great spice mix to ward off viral infections.

All health magazines have been promoting quinoa as a superfood. Quinoa is a pseudocereal, i.e., it is cooked and eaten like a cereal, but it is actually a seed. There are many not-so-popular cereals that can give quinoa a run for its money. Red and black rice grown in north–east India are loaded with antioxidants. Similarly, the millets that are peculiar to the Indian region – ragi, bajra, jowar – are rich in micronutrients. Moreover, these millets are richer in iron, protein and fibre as compared to wheat and rice, the staple grains. Ragi is a cereal that can compare with milk with respect to its calcium content.

There are many varieties of green chillies that are grown all over India. The antibacterial and pain-reducing abilities of chillies are well known, which is why it is fine if children consume a small amount of chillies.

Tamarind (*imli*) is yet another food that has been part of our diets but has not received its due. The power of tamarind lies in its antibacterial properties. It is a potentially cholesterol reducing agent (due to the high pectin content). In ancient Indian texts, it has been described as a fever reducer (the equivalent of the modern-day paracetamol). The ability of tamarind to retard kidney stone formation is yet another reason to include it in the diet.

The moot point here is that all vegetable-based foods are composed of hundreds of compounds. Many of these are yet unknown. This is why the potential to achieve superfood status is perhaps lying dormant in numerous foods. Let us wait and watch and, in the meantime, enjoy the benefits of what we already know by incorporating a variety of plant-based foods in our kids' diets in interesting ways.)

THE PERFECT SNACK

Sweet potato is considered a superfood packed with nutrients. One of the richest sources of beta-carotene comparable to that found in leafy vegetables, it is also a great source of Vitamin C and Vitamin B_6. An unique protein has been discovered in it that has cancer-fighting properties.

The reality is that we tend to make a new list of superfoods every year, leading to confusion. With regard to GM (Genetically Modified) foods, there are three points of view. For instance, the FDA, US, supports the use of GM foods whereas the American Academy of Environmental Medicine suggests issuing health warnings against GM foods, and the WHO believes in product-by-product assessment for GM foods.

[17]

The 20/20 Action Plan

The *European Journal of Prevention Cardiology* (2013) clearly cites that the next generation is expected to experience poorer health than the current one and the primary reason for that is the inferior lifestyle. This disturbing warning set me working on a practical and easy route to 'healthilicious' living. Each year has its fair share of novel diets that remain on top of the charts only to be replaced by another one very soon. However, the new era is not one of yo-yo diets but of healthy eating, which is simply about mindful eating plans.

Food for Thought

As this book is primarily meant for children, my approach to getting them to enjoy eating right is quite different from that for an adult. In fact, psychologists believe that if children are habitually forewarned about certain foods (oil-laced snacks and processed foods, for instance) they tend to have them with extra enthusiasm! Denial is obviously not the answer.

Evidently, constant disciplining may not work effectively for children, but consciousness and awareness does. When the child is very young, the parent has to take the lead. After all, will you not stop your child from poking his/her finger into the power socket? And on the same lines, will you knowingly offer harmful foods to young children? As they grow up, the goal of parenting would be to empower and help children to self-regulate their eating habits based on the structure that has been formulated by you over the years. The role of the parent changes to that of a mentor and guide over time.

I have noticed that despite the sincere desire and effort of parents to get children to eat well, the task can be daunting. That's why I have the 20-/20 Action Plan set out for you.

The 20/20 Action Plan

Quite like the perfection of 20/20 vision, this plan offers a simple, holistic approach to getting your child to eat right. After all, the perfect meal is much more than just the food on the plate. What you do before and after the meal is what completes it and makes it wholesome. Here are 20 practical recommendations to help you and your child get the best from food.

1 **Set your goal:** The idea is to make sure that your child eats healthy food. But it is also equally important that he/she enjoys the food that he/she eats. Eating with pleasure promotes healthy changes in the mind and the body.

2 **Plan the meal:** When working out meal menus, keep in mind the three principles of good eating practices, which are adequacy (enough to eat), variety (plenty of colours and textures) and balance (cover all food groups in the day for a balance of nutrients).

3 **Involve and engage kids** in the food they eat, in planning the meal and deciding what to eat. Go grocery shopping together. Play a game of spotting healthy foods and they will start reading labels before you know it.

4 **Shop smart:** Be price- and nutrient-wise. Many inexpensive foods can be more nutrient dense than the expensive ones.

5 **Hygiene:** Washing hands with soap before eating and preparing meals is an effective way of reducing microbial contamination. It is also crucial to wash/disinfect food items in the recommended way (see Chapter 6, *Washing and Storage*).

6 **Storage:** There are many different ways to store both both raw and cooked foods so as to prevent spoilage, and preserve and enhance nutrient worth.

7 **Cook and serve with happy feelings:** The '*haath ka khana*' is always tasty. The dose of love added to it makes a difference.

8 **Cookware/serving material:** Choose china, steel and glass over plastics for serving and cooking.

9 **Enhance the nutrients:** There are many ways to enhance the nutritive value of foods. Some processes are fermentation, sprouting, adding seeds to dough and batter, and so on.

10 **Minimize losses:** Don't overcook, as it causes nutrient loss. Fruit seeds and peels have immense nutritional worth. Leaves such as bay leaves and curry leaves are both edible and very valuable. So think before you discard seeds, peels and leaves.

11 **Best combinations of food groups:** Certain pairings of foods such as a cereal with a pulse are not just tasty but also complement each other in terms of the nutrients that they offer. Another worthy combination is iron and Vitamin-C-rich foods.

12 **Food presentation:** Just a topping of nuts or cherries, or serving the food item in interesting-looking crockery, can make a simple dish look extraordinary. Natural colours of food add appeal.

13 **Water/Hydration:** Giving children the right fluids in appropriate amounts is important, as they can often mistake thirst for hunger.

14 **Bond and eat together:** Eating together at the dining table is a great way to get the child to understand the importance of meal timings. Following some sort of routine and eating in appropriate positions (as opposed to eating in bed and the like), make a difference to the child's health). Food discipline begins this way. Allowing children to eat whatever and wherever they like is only going to harm them in the long run.

15 **Lead by example:** Non-verbal clues that children pick up at the dining table are usually much more important than what you tell them verbally. Your model of food acceptance is being watched all the time. Your personal prejudices towards certain foods easily register with children.

By eating a variety of foods slowly and mindfully yourself, you encourage the same behaviour in your child.

16 **Perfect the eye for portion sizes:** We tend to either overdo or underestimate portion sizes for children. An appropriate understanding of portion size can impact health for life.

17 **The right attitude towards food:** Unhealthy relationships with food can lead to eating disorders and poor body image. Undue restrictions can deprive the body of essential nutrients, and this can have an escalating impact as one grows older.

18 **Enjoy textures and different courses of the meal:** Finger foods are a good way to teach children about textures. It also helps them develop good motor skills. Allow your child to eat himself/herself, as this promotes a greater sense of satisfaction and satiety in him/her. It is also a good strategy to begin the meal with the least-liked food and end with the favourites.

19 **The home environment:** A healthy and relaxed supportive environment at home nourishes both physical and emotional well being. It influences the child's eating habits as well. More importantly, the kind of foods that one stocks at home will influence what the child begins to prefer and snack on. If, for some reason, you have stocked not-so-healthy foods, keep them away from direct sight.

20 **Be realistic:** Stay practical. Small mediated changes go a long way – quit the zero or hundred approach.

Healthy eating is more than just measuring food and counting calories. Follow these 20/20 guidelines and stay the course.

[18]

Empowering Meal Plans

The truth is, as a parent I know that sometimes even when you have the information, it is not always easy to apply that knowledge practically and that, too, day after day. That's why I have worked out meal plans that you can use instantly! Remember, these are templates to help you and not hard-and-fast rules.

Quite unlike the meal plans that are widely available, the ones that I have suggested are not in the least prescriptive. Strict and inflexible meal plans often limit the scope for you to incorporate the foods that you prefer and have easy access to. For instance, in the summer season in India, it is advisable to go for mangoes and the variety of melons available rather than an exotic variety of kiwi or passion fruit imported from across hundreds of miles. Moreover, meal plans that prescribe specific or exotic varieties of food are designed in a way to make you dependent on them. My meal plans, on the other hand, enable and empower you to make the right food choices by allowing you to pick the foods that you most enjoy and find easily at local stores.

So remember not to treat this plan as sacrosanct but just as a sample. Many of us need a wee bit of handholding before going full steam ahead. As long as one ensures that foods from all the essential food families (in the natural, unprocessed form) are included in the daily diet, one will not falter.

At the outset, let me tell you that the following two conditions have very little to do with the measure of both nutritional value and the taste of food:

- Exotic or fancy ingredients and elaborate cooking procedures can very well be done without.
- A meal with only one or two dishes (of the right combination) is just as good as a six-course meal. Appropriate planning is all-important. For instance, many one-pot dishes incorporate foods from three or four of the food families – this is quite enough for one meal. However, for packaged food, read the labels well so that your food quantity is regulated.

Some Empowering Points

- The information on exchanging one food for another within the same family (i.e., providing roughly the same nutritional value) is given in detail earlier Chapter 3, *The Truth about Portion Size*. Such exchange information will assist you in determining exact portions that should be used when substituting one kind of food for another. For instance, for practical purposes, fruits and vegetable are interchangeable. Thus, swapping fruits for vegetables and vice versa is allowed. This makes the goal of 'five a day' (eating five portions of fruit and vegetables per day) easier to achieve.

- As far as grains are concerned, try to include a variety from this family, keeping in mind that whole grains should be preferred. Another method of safeguarding a reasonable healthy cereal intake is to consume at least half the quota of grains required as whole grains (not the refined, processed variety).

Children have special requirements according to their age: In technical terms, children between 6 months to 2 years of age are referred to as infants and young children. Preschool children are those between 2+ to 5 years, older children are 5+ to 10 years, and the adolescent age group is 10+ to 19 years.

My book deals with children from one to 19 years. I had mentioned earlier in the book that at age one, the child should be eating the family meal, with appropriate modifications, to meet the nutrients required at this stage.

Age 1 to 2 years

Keep in mind the following points for this age group:

- Maintain food hygiene by washing hands and food products properly.
- Three small meals with two snacks are usually required because of the small appetite of young children.
- Do not force-feed the child under any circumstances. Alternative foods from the same food family, with

different textures and different combinations may work better, so give them a try.

- Foods that the children can pick up and eat themselves, such as cooked carrot cubes and potato wedges, should be included.
- Avoid adding excess salt and sugar to any of the foods.
- Introduce new foods one at a time with a gap of a few days between each.
- Do not confuse the child by offering too many flavours all at one meal.
- If the child is suffering from diarrhoea/vomiting, it is crucial to modify the diet and seek medical advice. There is no reason to stop food and starve the child. Avoid juices if the child is suffering from diarrhoea.

In one day, a 1 to 2-year-old needs:
Grains: 2–3 servings, **Vegetables:** 1–2 servings, **Fruit:** 1–2 servings, **Legumes:** ½ serving/50g **Meat**, **Milk:** 3 servings, **Fat:** 2–3 servings.

	Breakfast	Snack	Lunch	Snack	Dinner
MONDAY	½ cup milk ½ cup *poha*	1 Neer Dosa ½ cup fruits	1 cup Orange Punch ½ cup Yummy Macaroni with veggies	½ cup yogurt 1 Funky Cutlet	½ cup vegetable *khichri* ¼ cup White Islands
TUESDAY	¼ cup scrambled paneer	1 cup cut fruits	1 cup curd-rice ½ papad	2 Triple-S Sticks	1 Power-puff Idli

* See the *Recipes* section for the recipes whose initial letters are capitalized

	Breakfast	Snack	Lunch	Snack	Dinner
	½ Tri-Coloured Paratha				½ cup sambar
WEDNESDAY	½–1 cheese/ paneer toast ½ cup fresh juice	½ cup veg *upma* ½ cup lassi	½ *aloo* paratha ½ cup Dream Dal; ½ cup Spina-chips	1–2 Golden Diamonds ½ cup milk	½ cup Soy Ahoy Rice ½ cup vegetable curry
THURSDAY	1 cup Goldilocks Porridge	½ cup fruit juice 1 Super-licious Sesame Bar	½–1 roti 1 cup egg/ paneer curry	½ cup lassi 1 Sand Dune	1 cup vegetable – dal porridge 1 Date Lollipop
FRIDAY	1 Hearty Cutlet ½ cup yogurt	1 cup Chocomil Shake	1 veg paratha ½ cup peas curry	½ cup fruit 1 boiled egg	½ cup Pearly Snack ½ cup fruit raita
SATURDAY	1 Power-puff Idli ½ cup sambar	1 slice Banana-raga Bread ½ cup milk	½ cup Noobro Soup ½ Garlic-Basil Bruschetta	1 Faux Kebab ½ cup milk	½ cup Foxnut Curry ½–1 *suji cheela*
SUNDAY	½–1 Pretty Perfect Pancake ½ cup milk	1–2 Hearty Cutlets	½ cup rice ½ cup Coco Fish/ Paneer	1 Yum Yam Kebab ½ cup lassi	½ cup Carrot-Lentil Soup ½ cup Quick-Trick Quinoa

Age 2+ to 5 years

For the preschooler, too, follow the small meal pattern, that is, 3 meals and 2 snacks. Snacks play the important role of covering any gaps in nutrient intake.

- Provide as diverse a range of foodstuffs as possible as tastes developed at this stage will stay on for life.
- No force-feeding. Respect your child's hunger and fullness signals.
- The importance of breakfast should be emphasised at this stage itself.
- Water is best offered after a meal. Avoid colas, sweet beverages and fruit drinks.
- Make sure they wash their hands before eating. This practice has the power to save lives!
- Sugar intake should be minimal.

The nutritional requirement for the 2+ to 5-year-old age group goes up only slightly. A small increase in cereal, legume and fat servings is all that is needed to meet the requirement.

In one day, a 2+ to 5-year-old needs:
Grains: 3–5 servings, **Vegetables:** 1½–2 servings, **Fruits:** 1½–2 servings, **Milk:** 2–3 servings, **Legumes:** ¾–1 servings, **Fat:** 2–4 servings.

Use the same plan as that for 1–2-year-olds with additional servings as recommended.

Age 5+ to 10 years

Children in this age group keenly watch the food habits of the adults in the family. It is important to be a good role model.

- Make it a point to eat at least one meal of the day together as a family.
- Avoid watching television while eating meals/snacks.
- Involve your child in shopping, planning and execution of meals. Some recipes provided in the book are those that children enjoy making themselves (see under 'Cooking for Fun' in the *Recipes* section). Some sort of parental guidance while they cook can go a long way in developing their healthy interest in food.
- Packed lunch/tiffin-box menus should be prepared in consultation with the kids in this age group.
- Breakfast is crucial because it affects concentration levels at school.
- Water and not juices should be used to quench thirst.
- Iron-rich vegetarian sources should be served along with Vitamin C sources to enhance absorption, e.g., spinach with lemon dressing/lemonade.

In one day, a 5+ to 10-year-old needs:

Grains: 8–11 servings, **Vegetables:** 3 servings, **Fruits:** 2–3 servings, **Milk:** 2 servings, **Legumes/Meat:** 2 servings, **Fat:** 3–4 servings, **Sugar:** Up to 2–3 servings are acceptable.

	Breakfast	Tiffin	Lunch	Snack	Dinner
MONDAY	1 cup Grain-Wise Granola 1 cup milk	1 Best Bean Burger	2 Wow Wraps 1 cup fruit	1 cup Mint Amla Cooler 1 cup corn	1 cup Tangy Chickpeas 2–3 rotis ½–1 cup Saffron Green Salad
TUESDAY	1 cup Orange Punch 2–3 Super-licious Sesame Bar	2 mini No-bake Pizzas	1 cup veg noodles 1 cup Tomato Tofu	1 cup Date Smoothie 2–4 Funky Cutlets	1–2 cup peas pulao 1 cup YoYo Yogurt 1 cup Fruit Kebabs
WEDNESDAY	1 cup almond milk 2–4 Golden Diamonds 1 cup fruit	4–6 Triple-S Sticks with Blushing Dip	1 cup tomato rice 1 cup Lentil-Soya Discs 1–2 Jaggery Nut Chocolate	1 cup Pearly Snack 1 cup Water-melon Mocktail	2 Garlic-Basil Bru-schettas 1 cup Lemony Mush-rooms ½ cup Red Velvet Salad
THURSDAY	3–4 Energy Bites 1 cup fruit yogurt	3–4 Funky Cutlets with Greek Dip	2–3 paneer-stuffed roti 1 cup any lentil 1 cup seasonal veggies	1 cup fruit *chaat* ½ cup Maha Munchies	2 Tri-Coloured Paratha 1 cup yogurt ¼ cup Dark Knight

	Breakfast	Tiffin	Lunch	Snack	Dinner
FRIDAY	2 Choco Waffle Surprise 1 cup milk	2–3 Healthy Samosas with green chutney	1 Quick Quesa-dillas 1 cup Fruit Pops	1 cup fruit ¼ cup mixed nuts	1 cup veg biryani 1 cup Lentil-Soya Discs 1 slice Surprise Choco Cake
SATURDAY	2 Pretty Perfect Pancakes 1 cup fruit	1 cup Yummy Macaroni 2 Yum Yam Kebabs	2–3 garlic toast 1 cup Finger-lickin' Ladyfinger ½ cup cottage cheese patty	1 cup Coco Pina ½ cup veg sticks with Greek Dip	1 cup Carrot-Lentil Soup 1–2 dosas/ 1 cup *upma* 1 cup sambar + Red Chutney
SUNDAY	1 Wow Wrap 1 cup Watermelon Mocktail	2 Faux Kebab rolls	1 cup green rice 1 cup kidney beans ½ cup Cauliflower Salad	2 Potato Boats 1 cup milk-shake	2 Hunger-Buster Sandwiches 1 cup Spina-chips 1 Orange Cheese-cake Indica

Age 10+ to 19 years

Similar to the 0–2 year phase, there is a growth spurt at this age. For girls, this happens around 11–12 years, and for boys it is a little later, around 14 years. During the growth spurt in the adolescent phase, sudden weight gain (around 5 kgs) and height gain (around 5–6 cms per year during this growth phase of around three years) make the children vulnerable to eating disorders. Chronic problems such as anaemia and weak bones that are likely to develop at this stage can have serious implications later in life. Remember the following points:

- Physical activity that kids enjoy has to be inbuilt into their busy routines. Dear parents, just one hour a day in a 24-hour schedule is not difficult to achieve at all.
- Do not stock sugar-laden beverages and highly refined foods at home. Healthy snacks (foods that are not processed) should be easily accessible at home.
- Eating breakfast should be a non-negotiable issue. The usual excuses that children make should be foreseen and counter-arguments built up in favour of breakfast.
- It may be highlighted at this point that an adolescent child need not necessarily follow a five-meal pattern, which is required in the younger age group. A three- to four-meal pattern also works fine for them as their lives begin to get inundated with academic and extracurricular activities.
- It is also acceptable from the nutritional standpoint that meals and snacks get swapped, or at times even clubbed together, due to paucity of time.
- Desserts have not been included in the meal plan but can be added to the menu in acceptable portion sizes.

In one day, a 10+ to 19-year-old needs:

Grains: 12–16 servings, **Vegetables:** 2–3 servings, **Fruits:** 2–3 servings, **Milk:** 2 servings, **Legumes/Meat:** 2–3 servings, **Fat:** 5–8 servings, **Sugar:** Up to 3–4 servings are acceptable.

	Breakfast	Mid-morning	Lunch	Evening	Dinner
MONDAY	1 cup Chocomil Shake 2 Wow Wraps	3 Power-puff Idlis with chutney	1–2 cups rice with nuts 1 cup Tomato Tofu 2 Fruit Pops	1 cup banana smoothie 4–6 Momo Makeover	4 rotis 1 cup Nutty Aubergine 1 cup salad with Healthy Mayo
TUESDAY	1 cup lassi 2–3 lentil pancake (*cheela*), chutney	2–3 Choco Waffle Surprise 1 cup fruit	1–2 cups spinach rice 1 cup Shroomato 2 Jaggery Nut Chocolates	2 stuffed potatoes 1 cup Coco Pina	2–3 egg paratha 1 cup spicy pineapple curry
WEDNESDAY	1 cup almond milk 3–4 Energy Bites	4–5 Triple-S Sticks with Romesco Sauce	1 cup Coola Soupa 1 cup White Islands 2–3 flaxseed rotis	1 cup Orange Punch 1 cup Methi Mathri Chaat	1–2 cups Soy Ahoy Rice 1 cup YoYo Yogurt ½ cup Super Strong Salad

	Breakfast	Mid-morning	Lunch	Evening	Dinner
THURSDAY	1 cup Date Smoothie 2 Mintnut Sandwiches	2 Quick Quesedillas	1 cup black *chana* pulao 1 cup fruit raita	1 cup One Potato Two Potato with Blushing Dip 1 cup Water-melon Mocktail	1 cup vegetable noodles 1 cup vegetables in almond/ peanut sauce ½ cup Red Velvet Salad
FRIDAY	1 cup Grain-Wise Granola 1 cup yogurt	2 Hunger-Buster Sand-wiches	1 cup tamarind rice 1 cup mixed lentil ½ cup fruit raita	1 cup cold chocolate shake Chaat in a Cone	1 cup soya/ *keema* pasta 1 cup Saffron Green Salad 1 slice Surprise Choco Cake
SATURDAY	1 cup vanilla milk 2–3 French toasts	5–6 Momo Makeover 1 cup fruit nut salad	3 sprouted dal parathas 1 cup carrot raita	2 Pretty Perfect Pancakes 1 cup fruit	1 cup raisin rice 1 cup White Islands

	Breakfast	Mid-morning	Lunch	Evening	Dinner
			1 Orange Cheesecake Indica		1 cup veggies with Romesco Sauce
SUNDAY	1 cup hot cocoa 1 cup sprouts *upma*/ quinoa	2 Faux Kebabs/ Roti wrap	1 cup noodles 1 cup sweet-sour tofu/ paneer 1 cup Nutty Aubergine	1 cup Mint Amla Cooler 1 Best Bean Burger	3–4 green peas rotis 1 cup Pepper Chicken/ Pepper Mush-rooms 1 cup Red Velvet Salad

SECTION 7

RECIPES FOR MEALTIMES AND MORE

[19]

Recipes

Now that you know what to include in your child's diet, here is a selection of delicious and nutritious recipes to put your menu plans into action. The next set of pages have easy-to-make recipes for busy parents, to ensure the best of nutritional value and taste. These recipes are designed, keeping in mind what young, easily bored palates go for. Happy cooking!

Breakfast

Energy Bites

This recipe requires no cooking and features all healthy ingredients. Simply mix all the ingredients together. The perfect recipe to involve the kids in measuring and mixing.

Makes 40 bite-sized portions ■ *Prep time: 15 mins*

1 cup quick oats (dry roasted)
1¼ cup peanuts, coarsely pounded
¾ cup honey
1 cup fresh coconut, grated
½ cup flaxseeds, ground as a coarse powder
½ cup dark chocolate, grated coarsely or blended coarsely
½ tsp vanilla extract/essence
¼ cup milk powder

- Measure all the ingredients and mix well in a large bowl.
- Keep this mixture in the fridge for 10–15 minutes so that it becomes slightly firm.
- Shape the mixture into small bite-sized pieces. Place them in the freezer, to make them firmer.
- Dust with grated coconut.

Tip: The Energy Bites are ready to eat, but can be stored in the freezer, too. They make for a good snack option as well.

Golden Diamonds

Here's a quick and simple recipe that lets your child have the best of taste, too.

Makes 8–10 large diamonds ■ Prep time: 10 mins ■ Cook time: 15 mins

1 cup gram flour (*besan*)
1½ cup water
Salt to taste

For the tempering
½ tsp oil
1 tsp mustard seeds
1 tsp curry leaves
½ tsp chilli powder (optional)

- Use a thick, heavy-bottomed pan for this preparation.
- Mix the *besan* and water to make a paste. Add salt and mix. Pour into the pan.
- On a low flame, keep stirring the mixture in the pan till the mixture gathers together in the centre and turns into a ball.
- Pat this mixture into a deep plate (*thali*) and allow to cool for half an hour. Cut into diamond shapes.
- Heat the oil in a pan and add mustard seeds, chilli powder and chopped curry leaves and allow to cook for a minute. Pour this mixture over the *besan* diamonds and serve with a chutney of your choice.

Tip: Add ½ cup curd to the besan*–water and water mixture for some taste and texture variation.*

Superlicious Sesame Bars

One should not simply be counting calories while feeding kids. It is crucial to base the recipe on healthy ingredients.

Makes 22–25 bars ■ Prep time: 15 mins ■ Baking time: 15–20 mins

¾ cup jaggery
1 cup oatmeal/cornflour
½ cup sesame seeds
½ cup flaxseeds, ground
¼ cup soya flour
1–2 tbsp oil/butter
½ tsp baking soda
½ tsp baking powder

- Place the jaggery in a pan with ¼ cup water. Allow the jaggery to dissolve completely. If required, heat on a low flame to dissolve the jaggery.
- Mix the rest of the ingredients in a bowl.
- Now add the jaggery water to the dry ingredients and knead to form the dough.
- Divide the dough into small bar shapes.
- Bake on a slightly greased baking tray in an oven at 180°C for 15–20 minutes, until slightly brown.
- Cool and store in an airtight container.

***Tip:** You could sprinkle a little powdered sugar before serving to disguise the colour of the jaggery and flaxseeds.*

Powerpuff Idlis

This recipe does not require the usual ingredients (rice/*suji*) to make the idlis. It is also a great way to get the kids to eat legumes happily.

Makes 32 medium idlis ■ Prep time: Overnight soaking+ 20 mins ■ Cook time: 15 mins

1 cup *urad* dal
1 cup *moong* dal
1 tsp ginger paste
½ tsp black pepper powder
½ tsp turmeric powder
1 pinch of asafoetida (*hing*)
1 large lemon
1 tsp salt
½ pouch Eno salt (5g sachet), optional

- Soak both the dals overnight in adequate water. Drain out excess water and grind to a fine paste in a food processor.
- Leave covered to ferment for 12 hours. If there is no time for fermentation, mix in the Eno salt to help the batter to rise.
- Add turmeric, ginger paste, black pepper, asafoetida and salt to the fermented batter.
- Squeeze the juice of the lemon and add to the batter.
- Prepare *idlis* by steaming in the idli maker for 15 minutes.
- Remove from the moulds and cut into shapes of your choice.
- Serve with onion-tomato chutney or temper with mustard seeds and curry leaves.

Grain-Wise Granola

This recipe contains the goodness of grains and nuts combined. Honey and jaggery lend it a natural taste, too. It can be served with cold milk or yogurt as snack or a breakfast food.

Makes 3 cups ■ Prep time: 15 mins ■ Cook time: 40 mins

2 cups rice flakes, dry roasted in a skillet
1½ cup mixed nuts of your choice, chopped
1/3 cup honey
¼ cup jaggery, crumbled
1 tbsp cocoa powder
¼ cup olive/canola/rice bran oil
1 tsp roasted seeds

- In a wok, roast rice flakes over low heat for 5 minutes. Mix rice flakes and nuts in a bowl.
- In a pan, heat honey, powdered jaggery, oil and cocoa powder together. Cook on a low flame for 2 minutes till smooth. Pour this melted mixture over the dry ingredients (nuts and rice flakes) and mix well.
- Grease a baking tray. Spread the prepared mixture on it in a thin layer.
- Preheat the oven for 10 minutes. Put in the tray with the mixture and bake at at 120°C for 40 minutes. Stir once midway (after 15 minutes) through the baking process. Turn off the oven and allow the dish to cool before removing it from the tray. Store in an airtight container.

Tip: For classic granola, mix 3 cups oatmeal, 1 cup almonds, 1 cup walnuts, ¼ cup sugar, ¼ cup honey and ¼ cup olive oil, and bake as above.

Hummus Hunger-Buster Sandwich

Kids who don't like chickpea cooked in the traditional Indian style will enjoy this sandwich very much.

Makes 4 sandwiches ■ Prep time: 30 mins

1 cup boiled chickpeas
4 cloves garlic
1½ tbsp lemon juice
¼ tsp cumin powder
½ tsp salt
2/3 cup liquid leftover from boiling chickpeas
3 tbsp tahini paste (optional) (*recipe under Cauliflower Salad*)
1 tbsp virgin olive oil
4 slices wholegrain bread
2 tbsp shredded carrots

- In a food processor, add the boiled chickpeas along with the rest of the ingredients, i.e., garlic, lemon juice, cumin powder, salt and oil. It takes approximately 7–8 minutes to form a smooth paste.
- Once the paste is formed, add the leftover liquid preserved from the chickpeas to give the hummus the right consistency. Spread this on 4 slices of bread and garnish with shredded carrots.

Tip: You can think up interesting ways to present this sandwich, using other vegetables such as capsicum and edible leaves.

Goldilocks Porridge

Ramdana or *rajgiri* makes this dish rich in calcium, fibre and protein. The best part is that this porridge tastes like a dessert!

Serves 4 ■ Prep time: 10 mins ■ Cook time: 15 mins

½ cup amaranth seeds (*ramdana*)
½ cup oats
2 cups milk
1 cup grapes
1 tbsp honey
¼ tsp cinnamon powder
1 tsp lemon juice

- Boil the amaranth and oats in 1 cup milk. It takes about 10–15 minutes for the amaranth to cook to a soft, chewy state.
- Once cooked, add the rest of the milk. Water may be added during the cooking stage if the porridge becomes too dry even before it is cooked.
- Put grapes, honey, lemon juice and cinnamon powder in a separate pan. On medium heat, cook the above mixture for 5 minutes, while mashing it slightly with the back of a wooden spoon.
- Pour this fruit pulp on the boiled amaranth milk porridge.
- Serve it either hot or chilled.

Tip: You could substitute grapes with strawberries, blueberries or kiwi.

Quick-Trick Quinoa

This soft yet crunchy quinoa item is high on iron, calcium and protein.

Makes 2 cups ■ Prep time: 15 mins ■ Cook time: 20 mins

½ cup quinoa
2 bay leaves
1 pinch of mace (*jaiphal*)
1 large cardamom (black)
1 tbsp cooking oil
½ cup spinach/radish leaves
½ cup onions, chopped
1 tsp oregano/thyme/parsley
1 tsp mango powder (*amchur*)
Salt to taste
1 cup water

- Place the quinoa seeds in a sieve and rinse thoroughly under running water.
- Take 1 cup of water in a saucepan. Add ½ tsp salt along with bay leaves, mace and cardamom, and let it boil for 5 minutes. Strain the mixture to remove the whole spices, then put it back into the saucepan and allow it to simmer.
- Add the quinoa seeds and cook for 10 minutes. Drain off any excess water that remains after boiling and allow the quinoa to cool.
- In a skillet, take 1 tbsp oil and heat. Add spinach/radish leaves, chopped onions and spinach and cook for a minute. Add the cooked quinoa, oregano/thyme/parsley and the mango powder.
- Put the prepared portion into a greased steel mould (*katori*) and pack it in densely so that it takes the shape of the container. Invert the moulds gently after 15 minutes like one does with upside-down cakes and the quinoa cup is ready. Serve with a chutney of your choice.

***Tip:** Sprinkle coarsely ground peanuts over the quinoa cups and serve on a bed of kale/spinach leaves.*

Small Sand Dunes

Serves 2 ■ Prep time: 10 mins ■ Cook time: 15 mins

2 tbsp millet flour (ragi flour)
½ tsp baking powder
¼ tsp salt
2 eggs
4 egg whites
2 tbsp Cheddar cheese (or any hard cheese)
½ cup thick purée of vegetables (beans, cauliflower and carrot)
Oil for greasing the moulds

- Sift the flour with the baking powder and salt.
- Whisk the eggs (along with egg whites) in a bowl. Add the millet flour, cheese and the vegetable purée.
- Spoon this mixture into cupcake moulds that have been greased lightly.
- Bake at 200°C till the centre is cooked (approximately 15 minutes). Insert a toothpick and if it comes out clean, the puffs are ready.
- Remove from moulds and serve with garlic butter.

Lunch/Dinner

CEREALS

Tricolour Paratha

Here's a paratha with a blend of flavours, colours and nutrients.

Makes 10–12 parathas ■ Prep time: 20 mins ■ Cook time: 20 mins

For the dough:
750g wheat flour
1 large bunch spinach, blanched (approx. 250g)
250g carrots
1 cup beetroot
½ tsp carom seeds (*ajwain*)
½ tsp nigella sativa (*kalonji*)
Salt to taste
2½ tsp oil

- Blanch spinach. Remove excess water and grind. Purée carrots and beetroot separately with the least amount of water necessary.
- Divide the wheat flour into three parts. Mix one part with the spinach paste, in the second portion mix beetroot and, to the third, add carrot purée. If the carrots are not brightly coloured, you could add ¼ tsp turmeric powder.
- Add ½ tsp carom seeds, *kalonji* and salt to all the three portions and knead separately. There is usually no need to add extra water.
- Take three equal measures of all the three types of dough. Roll out each portion of the dough into a snake-like cylindrical shape.

- Place all the three dough-cylinders together (spinach and beetroot dough on either sides of the carrot one).
- Sprinkle with some dry flour and roll them all together in a spiral and make a ball.
- Flatten the ball into a circle of approximately 6" diameter. Repeat the same procedure for the entire dough.
- Heat the *tawa* and cook each paratha using ¼ tsp oil.
- Serve hot with chutney or any curry of your choice.

***Tip:** You could substitute spinach with any other season-appropriate leaves.*

Soy Ahoy Rice

Aroma and taste combine deliciously in this one-dish meal.

Makes 4 portions ■ *Prep time: 30 mins for soaking + 15 mins* ■ *Cook time: 20 mins*

1 cup rice (soaked for 30 mins), preferably the brown/red variety
½ cup soya granules
1 tsp oil
4 medium onions, sliced finely
1 tsp each of ginger and garlic paste
½ tsp chilli powder
2–3 pieces each of cloves, cardamom, black peppercorn, bay leaf
1 inch cinnamon stick
1 tsp cumin seeds
¼ cup yogurt
1 tsp coriander and mint leaves, chopped
1 tsp *kevda* (pandanus/screw-pine flower essence)
2 tbsp orange juice

- Cook the soaked rice in 3 cups of water till it is almost done. If white rice is used, 2 cups of water will suffice.
- Soak the soya granules in hot water for 15 minutes. Then squeeze out the excess water.
- In a *karahi*, heat 1 tsp oil, add the onions and cook till light brown. Remove half of the onions, for later use. To one part of the cooked onions, add ginger and garlic pastes, chilli powder, cloves, cardamom, black peppercorn, bay leaf, cinnamon stick and cumin seeds.
- Add the yogurt and cook for a few minutes. Next add the soya and cook for another minute.

- Add the soya mixture to the partially cooked rice along with the mint and coriander and *kevda*. Cover and cook till done. Add the orange juice. Top with the remaining browned onions. Serve with curry or yogurt.

Yummy Macaroni

In this recipe, chickpea adds not just to the nutrition but also to the texture and creamy consistency of the dish. Don't let the kids know what the secret of the creaminess is!

Serves 4 ■ Prep time: 10 mins ■ Cook time: 15 mins

1½ cup wholewheat macaroni
2 tsp oil (olive/rice bran/soya)
1 cup low-fat milk
½ cup cheese (Cheddar) grated
1 tsp cooking oil
½ cup boiled chickpea purée
1 tsp butter
4–5 cloves garlic, minced
1 bay leaf
¼ tsp salt
¼ tsp pepper, ground

- Boil water in a saucepan (about 2 litres). Add macaroni and salt and allow it to cook *al dente*, i.e., slightly undercooked. Drain and keep on a strainer/colander. Spread on a flat tray and sprinkle some oil on it so that the pasta does not stick together.
- Boil the milk with the bay leaf. Mix the chickpea purée to the milk and blend well.
- In a skillet, add the cooking oil and butter. Heat moderately, add minced garlic, the chickpea–milk mixture, grated cheese (in this order) and cook for 2 to 3 minutes. Add the macaroni and stir it. Add ground pepper and serve.

Pearly Snack

This dish is high on good carbohydrates that kids need in plenty. It's time to ditch the refined flours and switch to better alternatives.

Serves 4 ■ Prep time: 1 hr (including soaking time) ■ Cook time: 10 mins

1 cup sago (*sabudana*)
1 tsp oil
1 tsp fennel seeds
½ tsp cumin seeds
Salt to taste
50g roasted peanuts, broken up slightly
1 tbsp chopped coriander leaves
½ tsp sugar

- Soak the sago in water for 10 minutes. Drain the water and place the sago in a strainer/colander for another hour so that it remains moist. You could sprinkle water if the sago becomes dry.
- Heat the oil in a wok, add fennel seeds and cumin seeds, and allow to brown slightly. Add the soaked drained sago and cook till the sago turns translucent. Mix in peanuts, salt, sugar and coriander leaves. Serve with dollops of crunchy chutney.

Tip: Make the chutney by mixing drained thick curd, mint leaves, peanuts and green chilli. Add cumin powder and salt to taste.

Neer Dosa

This is a tasty, soft dosa that kids are sure to love.

Makes 6 dosas ■ *Prep time: 6 hours soaking + 10 mins* ■ *Cook time: 10 mins*

1 cup rice (any kind but not basmati)
½ cup coconut fresh, blended in a food processor
½ tsp salt
Water to make a thin flowing batter (of *rasam* consistency)

- Soak the rice in 5 cups of water and leave overnight. A minimum of 5–6 hours of soaking is required.
- Grind in the food processor to a fine paste.
- Grind the fresh coconut also to a fine paste. Blend into the rice paste.
- Heat a small non-stick pan on the stove, pour one ladle of the rice-coconut paste in the centre and by tilting the pan make sure that the batter spreads out into a thin circle.
- Cover and allow to cook for 2 minutes.
- When you notice that the edges of the dosa begin to curl up slightly, remove from the pan with a spatula.
- Fold like a hankerchief.
- Serve with tomato–onion chutney.

LEGUMES

Lentil-Soya Discs

This is a delicious substitute for *vadas*. It needs no frying but tastes just as good.

Makes 12 medium-size dumplings ■ Prep time: 6 hours soaking+ 10 mins ■ Cook time: 15 mins

250 g red lentils (*masoor* dal)
25g soya *keema*/granules (¼ of packet)
1 medium carrot, chopped
1 medium capsicum, chopped
1 tsp salt
1 tsp chilli flakes
½ Eno sachet (regular, no flavour)
2 cups yogurt
½ tsp cumin powder
1 tbsp curry leaves, chopped

- Soak the lentils in adequate water overnight or for a minimum of 6 hours. Drain excess water and grind to form a paste.
- Soak the soya granules in hot water for 10 minutes. Then squeeze out excess water from the granules.
- Mix the lentil paste and soya granules. Add the chopped carrot and capsicum, salt and chilli flakes, and blend into the mixture.
- Add ½ sachet of Eno salt to the batter and mix well.
- Place the idli maker on the stove with enough water to generate steam. When the water comes to a boil, grease the idli moulds and pour batter into them. Cook for 12 minutes.
- Remove from the moulds and cool. Cut into desired shapes.
- Blend yogurt, and add the chopped curry leaves,

cumin powder and salt to taste. This makes the sauce for the prepared discs. Add the discs to it and keep aside for 15 minutes.

- Serve as part of a main meal or as a snack.

Dream Dal

Dal Makhani is usually made using dollops of cream. This recipe requires no cream, and no frying of onions or tomatoes, but tastes just as delicious. Prepare the dal a day in advance and keep it overnight in the fridge. Serve it the next day to enjoy its rich flavour.

Makes 4 medium bowls ■ *Prep time: soak overnight + 10 mins* ■ *Cook time: 30 mins*

¾ cup black gram dal (whole *urad* dal)
2 tsp salt
3 tsp ginger paste
3 tsp garlic paste
¾ cup tomato purée
¼ tsp red chilli powder
2 tbsp butter

- Soak the dal overnight.
- Drain off the water and add fresh water (5 cups) and salt to the dal. Pressure cook till well-cooked (about 20 mins). Mash the cooked dal lightly with a wooden spoon.
- Add ginger paste, garlic paste, tomato purée, red chilli powder, butter and salt to taste. Cook for another 20–30 mins.
- Serve hot with rice/bread/roti.

Tangy Chickpeas

This recipe does not require tomatoes or garlic yet it tastes great. All the kids in my family love this preparation so much that they refuse to have chickpeas prepared in any other style.

Makes 4–6 portions ■ *Prep time: overnight soaking + 15 mins* ■ *Cook time: 15 mins*

1 cup white *chana* (soaked overnight)
4 medium onions, chopped finely
100g cilantro/coriander, finely chopped
3 tsp oil
¼ cup tamarind, soaked in 1 cup water
¼ cup jaggery, powdered
Salt to taste
2 green chillies, sliced or chopped

- Drain and cook the *chana* in 5 cups water in a pressure cooker (30 minutes).
- Once cooked, cool and retain the water that remains. This could be used to soak the tamarind.
- In a skillet, add oil and heat. Add the chopped onions and cook till transparent.
- Make a paste of the tamarind.
- Add the boiled chickpeas, tamarind paste, chopped coriander, jaggery and salt, and cook till all the items are mixed well. Add the green chillies.
- The chickpeas coated in the thick, sweet-sour sauce go well with rice as well as chapattis or bread.

VEG PROTEIN ALTERNATIVES

Shroomato

Shiitake mushrooms are known for their healing properties. Their immunity-boosting powers make them a very sought-after ingredient.

Makes 4 portions ■ *Prep time: 15 mins* ■ *Cook time: 15 mins*

1 tbsp oil
4–5 green chillies
1 medium onion, chopped
2 cups water
5 cloves garlic, crushed
2 medium tomatoes, chopped
50g grated cheese (feta/cottage/Cheddar)
100g shiitake mushrooms, chopped (dried mushrooms are soaked in hot water for 10 mins to rehydrate)
Few sprigs of fresh coriander

- In a pan, heat the cooking oil. Add the green chillies and onion, and cook for 2–3 minutes. Add water and allow it to boil.
- Add garlic and tomatoes and cook for another 2–3 minutes.
- Now add the grated cheese, chopped mushrooms, and cook briefly for a minute.
- Add sprigs of coriander and cover the dish for 5 minutes, allowing the flavours to be absorbed.
- Serve with brown rice or garlic toast.

Tip: You can use button mushrooms instead of shiitake mushrooms if availability is an issue. Wash and wipe the mushrooms dry. Chop into quarters before adding.

White Islands

Here's a simple and tasty paneer dish with a difference.

Makes 4 portions ■ *Prep time: 15 mins* ■ *Cook time: 20 mins*

200g paneer
4 tbsp thick curd
½ tsp ginger paste
½ tsp garlic paste
½ tsp turmeric
1 tsp oil
½ tsp *kasoori methi* (dried fenugreek))
½ tsp garam masala
Salt to taste

- Slice the paneer into rectangular, 1-inch thick pieces. Arrange in an ovenproof dish.
- Whip curd. Add ginger, garlic, turmeric, garam masala, *kasoori methi*, oil and salt and mix well. The yogurt sauce is ready.
- Spoon the sauce over and around the paneer pieces in the overnproof dish.
- Grill/bake in a moderate oven (180–200°C) till the sauce is slightly brown (approximately 15–20 minutes).

Tomato Tofu

Many kids do not like tofu, but in this recipe the taste of tofu is well masked by soya sauce and tomatoes.

Makes 4 portions ■ Prep time: 10 mins ■ Cook time: 10 mins

200 g tofu
2 tbsp soya sauce
2 tsp ginger–garlic paste
2 tsp oil
1 medium spring onion with leaves, shredded
3 medium tomatoes, blanched

- Mix the soya sauce and garlic-ginger paste with the tofu (cut in any desired shape) and leave for 15 minutes.
- Take oil in a skillet and add the marinated tofu and pan-fry till golden brown.
- Chop the blanched tomatoes finely. Add to the tofu along with the spring onion. Cook for 3–4 minutes and serve.

***Tip:** Roast 1 tbsp of sesame seeds in ¼ tsp oil (sesame/peanut/rice bran) and add as a topping.*

VEGGIES

Spinachips

Spinach leaves prepared this way are so crunchy and tasty that kids love them. They could add the crispy leaves to any dish or eat them as a snack. The same recipe can be followed for kale leaves to make a nutritious snack.

Makes 25 pieces ■ *Prep time: 20 mins* ■ *Cook time: 10 mins*

20–25 spinach/kale leaves (small-sized)

1 tsp olive oil/sesame oil

2 tsp sesame seeds

- Wash and dry spinach/kale leaves by wiping them with a cloth. If the leaves are not dried well, the chips will turn out soggy.
- Preheat oven at 175°C for 10 minutes.
- Brush the leaves with a thin layer of oil and place on a baking tray.
- Bake for 7–10 minutes, turning the leaves over (halfway through the baking) so that they are evenly done.
- Sprinkle salt and a spice of your choice, which could be black pepper, curry powder or *chaat* masala, and sesame seeds.

Tip: If the kale leaves are large, the main rib should be removed and the leaves torn into 1–1½ inch pieces.

Finger-lickin' Ladyfinger

Most kids like *bhindi* only when it is deep-fried. Here's an entirely different way of serving it – appetizing yet healthy.

Serves 4 ■ Prep time: 30 mins ■ Cook time: 15 mins

250 g *bhindi*
½ cup vinegar
1 tsp salt
3 medium onions, sliced
4 tsp olive/sesame oil
1 tsp garlic, minced
4 medium tomatoes, grated
3 tbsp tomato purée or paste
Salt and pepper to taste
1 tsp sugar
2 tsp lemon juice
1 tbsp parsley/oregano dry flakes

- Remove the stems of the *bhindis* and place the *bhindis* in a bowl. Add vinegar and 1 tsp salt to it. Leave for half-hour and then drain. This helps to get rid of the sliminess.
- Heat oil in a skillet, add sliced onions and cook till they become soft but not brown. Add the *bhindis* and cook till they begin to change colour.
- Add minced garlic, cook and then add tomatoes. Cook till tomatoes become soft. Add tomato purée diluted in half cup water. Cook for one minute.
- Add salt, sugar and pepper to the above ingredients.
- Cover and cook till the *bhindis* are tender. Add lemon juice and parsley/oregano and cook for another minute. Serve with bread/roti of your choice.

Tip: Don't soak the bhindis *for more than 30 minutes or they will get mushy.*

Nutty Aubergine

My kids refused to eat aubergine until they tried this dish. Now, this is the only aubergine preparation acceptable at home.

Serves 4 ■ Prep time: 20 mins ■ Cook time: 15 mins

1 cup curd
1 tsp garlic paste
2 round aubergines
3 tsp oil

For red sauce
4 medium onions, chopped
2 tomatoes, chopped
5 tbsp peanuts
2 tbsp sesame seeds
Salt and chilli powder to taste

- Tie the curd in a muslin cloth to drain the water for one hour. Add garlic paste to the drained curd; mix well.
- Slice the brinjals into half-inch thick rounds and sauté in 1 tsp of oil in a non-stick pan. Remove from the pan and keep aside.
- In the same pan, with 1 tsp oil, sauté the onions till they turn translucent. Add chopped tomatoes, chilli powder and salt to it and make a mixture.
- Lightly roast the peanuts and sesame seeds on a *tawa* (without any oil) on a low flame, taking care not to overdo it. Put in a blender and make a paste. Mix it into the onion–tomato mixture. The red sauce is ready.
- Place the brinjal pieces on a serving dish and pour the prepared red sauce over it. Spoon out small portions of the yogurt–garlic paste and spread over the brinjal slices. Over the yogurt layer, add another layer of the red sauce and serve.

Foxnut Curry

The starchy white seeds of the water lily are eaten in many forms. This nut was also used in traditional Chinese medicine and is still regarded as an excellent source of starch for children.

Serves 4 portions ■ Prep time: 20 mins ■ Cook time: 10 mins

1 tsp oil
3/4 cup *makhanas* (foxnuts)
2 tbsp ginger–garlic paste
2 large onions, finely chopped
4 tomatoes, sliced
2 green chillies, sliced
1½ cup peas, boiled
2 tsp pepper powder
Salt to taste

- In a pan, take 1 tsp oil and lightly roast the foxnuts and keep aside.
- Heat 1 tsp oil in a wok and sauté the onions until they turn light brown.
- Add the ginger–garlic paste to it and sauté for another 2 mins.
- Add the green chillies and tomatoes, and continue to fry. Mix boiled peas and foxnuts, along with enough water to make the curry of a thin consistency.
- Cover and let it simmer for 5 minutes.
- Add salt and pepper, and serve.

***Tip:** The gravy for this dish is supposed to be slightly thin in consistency. A thick gravy will ruin the flavour of the dish.*

NON-VEGETARIAN RECIPES

Mutton Kashmere

Make red meat in this healthy, tasty way in a jiffy! This recipe does not require any onions or tomatoes.

Makes 4 portions ■ Prep time: 5 mins ■ Cook time: 25 mins

500g mutton or 8 small pieces
1½ tbsp mustard oil
1 tsp dry ginger powder
3 tsp fennel powder (*saunf*)
1 tsp cumin powder
3 bay leaves
4 pieces of clove
4 pieces of cardamom (black and green)
2 small sticks of cinnamon
500g yogurt
Pinch of asafoetida
Salt to taste

- Heat oil in a pressure cooker. When the oil is adequately heated, add asafoetida and stir for a few seconds.
- Add mutton pieces, and all the spices. Mix well.
- Cook for 20 minutes in the pressure cooker. Remove from heat.
- Blend the yogurt to make it smooth.
- Add the blended yogurt to the meat. Keep stirring and cooking over low heat until a small amount of gravy remains.
- Remove from heat. Serve with roti or rice.

Coco Fish

This dish is fun with fish, and for vegetarians one could substitute veggies, mushrooms or tofu for fish.

Serves 4 ■ Prep time: 15 mins ■ Cook time: 15 mins

500g fish fillet or 8 pieces (*singhara/basa/rohu*)
1½ tbsp oil
2 medium onions
1 tsp garlic, chopped
1 tsp ginger, chopped
2 green chillies (optional)
3 tbsp curry leaves, shredded (retain some for the garnish)
¼ tsp turmeric powder
1 cup coconut milk
Salt to taste

- Prepare the masala by grinding the onions, garlic, ginger, chillies, curry leaves and turmeric powder.
- Heat the oil in a pan. Add the ground onion masala and cook for 2–3 minutes.
- Add the poached fish fillets to the cooked onion masala and fry for another 2 minutes.
- Poach the fish fillets in boiling water for 5 minutes.
- Add the coconut milk and salt, and cover. Allow to simmer and cook for about 10 minutes.
- Garnish with shredded curry leaves and serve hot.

Tip: *It is good to eat a variety of fish instead of just one kind. A regular intake of fish, just 2–3 times a week, is good enough to provide the benefits.*

Pepper Chicken

Black pepper is a valuable spice. It is not only high on antioxidants but is also an immunity enhancer.

Serves 4 ■ *Prep time: 10 mins* ■ *Cook time: 25 mins*

1 tbsp oil
3 cloves
3 cardamoms
2 bay leaves
½ kg chicken (boneless) or 750g with bones
2 tsp ginger–garlic paste
1 cup thick curd
¼ tsp turmeric powder
1 tbsp peppercorn, crushed
½ tsp garam masala
2 tbsp ground cashewnut paste (soak the cashews in milk for 30 mins before grinding)
Salt to taste

- Heat oil in a pan. Add the whole spices (cardamoms, bay leaves and cloves) and stir till light brown.
- Add the chicken pieces and sauté. Next, add the ginger–garlic paste and cook for another minute.
- Add curd, turmeric powder, peppercorn and garam masala. Mix well, cover and cook on low heat till the chicken is cooked. (You may add ½–1 cup of water at this stage if the chicken seems to be getting too dry).
- Add the thick cashew paste and salt, and cook for another 5–8 minutes.
- Cover and allow the dish to sit for another 10 minutes before serving.

Tip: Do not exceed the specified amount of cashews for the paste as it will ruin the taste of the dish. Also, use freshly ground peppercorns as their flavour is more enhanced.

Momo Makeover

Makes 15 dumplings ■ Prep time: 30 mins ■ Cook time: 20 mins

For the shell

½ cup wheat flour

½ cup cornflour

1 egg

1 tbsp cooking oil

¼ tsp baking soda

For the filling

1 cup boneless boiled chicken

½ cup chopped onions

½ cup grated or shredded cabbage

6–7 garlic cloves, coarsely ground

1–2 green chillies (optional)

1 tbsp finely chopped coriander leaves

2 green chillies (optional)

1 tsp cooking oil (sesame/ peanut/rice bran)

1 tbsp soya sauce

Salt to taste

- Mix all the ingredients for the cover/shell and add water to make the dough soft. Cover and keep aside for 15 minutes.
- Mix all the ingredients for the filling in a separate bowl.
- In a skillet, heat the oil and sauté the veggies for 2 minutes on high heat. Then add salt to taste and the soya sauce.
- Divide the dough into 15 portions. Roll out the dough into very thin rounds.
- In the centre of the rolled-out dough, place a spoonful of the mixture prepared for the filling. Bring the edges together and twist to make a pouch.
- Steam in an idli stand placed in a pressure cooker for 4 whistles. Alternatively, use a rice steamer and place the idli stand in it. Cook in it for 10 minutes.

- The dumplings are ready to be served.

***Tip:** For vegetarians: In place of chicken, take ½ cup soya granules and soak in 1 cup warm water. Squeeze to remove excess water. Heat a pan with 1 tsp oil and cook the soya granules until absolutely dry. Use instead of chicken in the recipe.*

Desserts

Jaggery Nut Chocolate

This homemade chocolate is healthy. Children enjoy the goodness of jaggery and also stay off the not-so-healthy sweeteners added to commercially prepared products.

Makes 12 pieces ■ Prep time: 10 mins ■ Cook time: 5 mins

1 bar dark chocolate compound
½ cup jaggery, crumbled
¼ cup almonds or any other nut, chopped coarsely
A pinch of nutmeg (optional)

- Grate the chocolate compound coarsely.
- Put the grated chocolate in a microwave-safe glass container and heat for 30 seconds at full power. If you find that the chocolate has not quite melted, you could heat for an additional 10 seconds.
- Melt the crumbled jaggery on the stove on low heat. It takes about 1 minute to melt completely.
- Add the melted jaggery to the slightly melted chocolate compound.
- Add chopped nuts and stir well. Add nutmeg for a hint of spice, if you like.
- Spoon this mixture into silicone moulds. The batter should not overflow the moulds.
- Place the moulds in the refrigerator for 5 minutes to set the chocolate. Remove from moulds and serve.

Tip: This recipe is so simple that your kids would love to make it (under supervision).

Orange Cheesecake Indica

Make this indulgent dessert a guilt-free one. Your kids will enjoy this contemporary avatar of *sandesh*.

Makes 8 medium portions ▪ Prep time: 1 hr 15 mins ▪ Cook time: 10 mins

1 litre low-fat milk (double-/ single-toned)
2 tsp lemon juice
¼ tsp orange/lemon rind, grated finely
4 tsp powdered sugar
4 orange segments
1 tbsp biscuit crumbs/ 8 plain cookies

- Boil milk and add lemon juice. Once the milk starts to curdle, bring to a boil and turn off the heat.
- Leave the curdled milk in a fine strainer so that the whey water is completely drained (about 1 hour). Do not forcefully extract the water.
- Add powdered sugar and blend well (using the palm of the hand) with the cottage cheese extracted. Add orange/lemon rind for flavour.
- Place the cottage cheese in a thick-bottomed *karahi* and cook over low heat, mashing it gently with a wooden spoon for about 10 minutes. The cheesecake mixture is ready when the cottage cheese no longer looks sticky and grainy in texture. Allow to cool slightly.
- Divide the cooked cheese into 8 small portions and make balls. Place a small piece of orange segment at the centre of the ball and then reconstruct into a shape that you like. Dust with biscuit crumbs. Alternatively, serve the cheesecake on a cookie.

Sweet-Sour Sorbet

Unripe mangoes are an excellent source of Vitamin C, with an irresistible tang. Protection from sunstroke is just one of the health benefits of raw mango.

Makes 4 scoops ■ *Cook time: 15 mins* ■ *Freezing time: 1 hour*

8 medium-sized raw mangoes without removing the peel
2 tsp mint leaves chopped
4 tbsp brown sugar
¾ tsp black salt

- Cook the mangoes in 2 cups water in the pressure cooker for 5 minutes.
- Remove the mangoes from the water, remove the peel and scoop out the flesh.
- Put it in the blender along with the mint leaves till the mixture is smooth.
- Add sugar and salt to the mixture. Heat it in a pan over medium heat, till it reaches a thick creamy consistency.
- Freeze in a suitable container till it solidifies. Scoop out and serve in an ice-cream bowl.

Tip: *Use raw mango strips in salads, in sambar or add to rice along with herbs and spices.*

Carrot Cupcake

Barley flour and carrots combine to make these winning cupcakes. The kids get the benefit of the 'health food' – barley – without any fuss.

Makes 15 cupcakes ■ *Prep time: 20 mins* ■ *Cook time: 25 mins*

1½ cup barley flour
1 tsp baking powder
1 tsp baking soda
¾ tsp salt
¼ tsp grated nutmeg
¾ cup cooking oil
¾ cup brown sugar
1 large egg
2 tbsp yogurt
¼ tsp vanilla extract
1½ cups grated carrot (approx. 4 medium carrots)

Frosting

1 cup thick yogurt (water drained)
1 cup unsalted butter
½ cup brown sugar, ground
1 ½ tsp vanilla extract
1 tsp grated lemon zest

- In a bowl, mix together the flour, baking powder, soda, and salt, and set aside.
- In another bowl, mix oil, egg, brown sugar, yogurt and vanilla extract. Add the carrots to it. Add the dry ingredients to this and mix well.
- Pour into muffin tins after greasing them.
- Bake at 190°C for 20–25 minutes. Cool.
- Prepare the frosting by beating the yogurt with sugar and butter until smooth. Add vanilla extract and the lemon zest.
- Top the completely cooled cupcake with a layer of the yogurt frosting.

Dark Knight

This very healthy brownie – yes, there *is* such a thing – is the answer to all demands for confectionery.

Serves 6 ▪ Prep time: 30 mins ▪ Cook time: 45 mins

1 cup sorghum (jowar) flour
2 tsp baking powder
½ tsp salt
¾ cup brown sugar for batter + ¾ cup brown sugar (for sprinkling)

2 tbsp cocoa + ¼ cup cocoa (for sprinkling)
½ cup milk
1 tsp vanilla extract
2 tbsp oil/butter melted
1 cup chopped walnuts
1¾ cups hot water

- Sift together flour, baking powder, salt, sugar and cocoa.
- Add milk, vanilla extract and oil/butter until smooth. Add the walnuts.
- Pour the mixture into a greased 8-inch square cake pan.
- Mix brown sugar and cocoa and sprinkle it over the batter. Pour hot water over the entire batter.
- Bake in the oven at 175°C for 40–45 minutes.
- Serve warm.

Surprise Choco Cake (Eggless)

The alternatives to normal flour used in this cake and the surprise ingredients turn it into a very healthy proposition.

Makes 20 slices ■ Prep time: 15 mins ■ Cook time: 45 mins

1 ripe banana, mashed
1 cup cold milk (dairy/almond/coconut)
1¾ cup honey
2 tsp vanilla essence
1 1/3 cup almond flour (almond ground into a flour)
1 cup cornflour (*makki ka atta*) or wheat flour
¾ cup cocoa powder
2 tsp baking powder
A pinch of salt
¾ cup oil (coconut/canola/rice bran)

- Preheat the oven to 180°C.
- Add the mashed banana, honey and vanilla essence to the chilled milk and keep aside.
- Grease a baking pan with a removable base.
- Put the almond flour, cornflour, baking powder and salt in a bowl.
- Make a well in the centre. Pour oil and the milk-banana mixture into it and mix well.
- Transfer into the baking dish and bake for 45 minutes until done. Remove from pan.
- Slice and serve.

Date Lollipop

If your kids ask for more of this lollipop, you are going to be a happy parent, right? Dates are one of the most nourishing fruits and here is a way to get the kids to like them.

Serves 4 ■ Prep time: 20 mins

250g dates
2 tbsp cashewnuts
2 tbsp almonds
2 tbsp walnuts
2 tbsp edible gum/*gond katira*
2 tbsp poppy seeds (*khus khus*)
1 tbsp butter/ghee/oil
A pinch of nutmeg powder

- Deseed the dates, chop into large pieces and put in a blender to make a smooth paste.
- Coarsely chop the nuts (possible in a chilli cutter, too).
- In a wok, add 1 tbsp butter/ghee/oil and heat. Add the gum pieces and allow it to cook.
- Remove the cooked gum pieces from the wok.
- Add the poppy seeds and date mixture to the same and mix well.
- Add nutmeg powder and nuts, and mix well. Make small round shapes of the mixture.
- Stick the rounds onto ice-cream sticks or thin bamboo sticks to make them look like lollipops, and serve.

SALADS

Ruby Salad

A combination of a fruit and a legume, this high-energy salad can be served as a snack as well.

Serves 4 ■ Prep time: Overnight (soaking) + 15 mins

2 tbsp black chickpea, boiled (*kala chana*)
2 medium potatoes
1 cup pomegranate seeds
1 tsp lemon juice
1 tsp roasted cumin powder
Salt to taste

- Soak the black chickpea overnight in water and pressure cook for 10 minutes.
- Boil the potato separately.
- Peel and chop the potato and mix with the *chana* and pomegranate seeds.
- Add the lemon juice, salt and cumin powder. Mix well and it's ready to serve.

Red Velvet Salad

A substantial salad that will add a lot of goodness to your child's menu.

Serves 2 ■ Prep time: 15 mins

2 medium beetroot
1 egg, hard-boiled
½ onion, finely chopped
2 tbsp French dressing (equal parts of lemon juice and oil, mixed)
½ tbsp coriander leaves, chopped

- Cook the beetroot in a pressure cooker for 10 minutes. Cool and peel. Dice the beetroot.
- Slice the boiled egg into half and remove the yolk. Chop the egg white finely.
- Mix together the diced beetroot, sliced onions and egg white.
- Rub the yolk through a metal strainer so that it is evenly crumbled, and add to the mixture.
- Pour the French dressing over it.
- Sprinkle the chopped coriander leaves over the salad and it's ready to serve.

Tip: To cook the beetroot, you could also bake the beetroot as one bakes potato. For the presentation, especially for younger kids, you could make a 'funny face', using pieces of the boiled egg whites for eyes, beetroot for the nose, and leaves for the mouth.

Saffron Green Salad

Forget the nutrients, just the colours of this salad will get the kids going for it.

Serves 2 ■ Prep time: 15 mins

½ cup spinach leaves (1 small bunch)
1 cup oranges (2 medium)

For the dressing
4 dates
2–3 walnuts
½ inch piece of ginger
A pinch of saffron
1 tsp soya sauce
Salt to taste

- Wash the spinach and cut into strips with a pair of scissors.
- Deseed the oranges.
- Prepare the dressing by mixing all the ingredients for the dressing in the blender.
- Pour the dressing over the spinach and orange just before serving.
- Serve chilled.

Cauliflower Salad

We often presume that rich dressings in salads incorporate lots of cream. This recipe uses sesame to create the same taste!

Serves 2 ■ Prep time: 15 mins

2 cups cauliflower flowerets, steamed

For tahini paste
2 tbsp sesame seeds
½ tsp sesame/olive oil
¼ cup warm water
2 tbsp lemon juice
5–6 cloves garlic, minced
Salt to taste

- Grind the sesame seeds, oil and salt in the blender. Add the warm water gradually in small amounts and continue to blend till a smooth paste results (approx. 5 minutes). Pour into a bowl and add minced garlic and lemon juice.
- Pour this paste over the steamed cauliflower and mix well.
- Chill and serve.

Tip: Toast a slice of readymade pizza base or pita bread and place the salad on it. Garnish with tomato ketchup/chutney.

Soups

Noobro Soup

Noodles and broccoli combine to make a dish you never thought your kids would love!

Makes 4 cups ■ Prep time: 10 mins ■ Cook time: 15 mins

1 cup chopped broccoli (head along with peeled soft stems)
2 cups milk
2 tsp butter/olive oil
1 medium onion, finely chopped
Salt and pepper to taste
½ cup boiled noodles (any wholegrain noodles)

- Heat 1 tsp of butter/olive oil in a pan. Add the chopped broccoli and cook for 7–8 minutes till the broccoli is slightly soft.
- Add the milk to the cooked broccoli and cook for a few minutes again.
- In a separate pan, heat 1 tsp butter and add the finely chopped onions. Cook till slightly brown and add to the broccoli–milk mixture.
- Grind this mixture in a blender for two minutes till it is of a soupy consistency.
- Top with boiled noodles, add salt and pepper, and serve hot.

Carrot-Lentil Soup

Carrots and dal – when your kids ask for more of this, you know you have made magic!

Makes 2 cups ■ Prep time: 20 mins ■ Cook time: 15 mins

1 tbsp red lentil (*masoor* dal)
¾ small apple
1 small carrot, chopped
1 tbsp red lentil (*masoor dal*)
½ small onion, chopped
1 tsp butter/oil
¼ tsp curry/sambar powder
2 cup vegetable stock/water
Lemon juice to taste
Sprig of parsley/coriander

- Soak the dal in water for 15–20 minutes.
- In a skillet, heat the butter/oil. Add to it chopped apple, carrot and onion. Cook for 2–3 minutes till the apples and onions turn slightly soft and translucent.
- Add curry/sambar powder to the above mix and stir well.
- Add the soaked dal along with the water/stock. Cover and allow it to simmer for 10 minutes. Blend and sieve.
- Add lemon juice and serve with a sprig of parsley/coriander and a sprinkling of chopped apples.
- Serve with boiled noodles.

Coola Soupa

Did you know that a generous intake of vegetables influences the bacteria in the gut, protecting us from infections?

Makes 1 large glass (300ml) ■ *Prep time: 10 mins*

100g cucumber, chopped
50g tomatoes, chopped
50g onions
1 tbsp lemon juice
1tsp butter/olive oil
1/3 tsp salt
3–4 mint leaves, shredded
½ cup water

- In a blender, place the chopped cucumber, tomatoes, onion, lemon juice and butter/olive oil and mint leaves. Blend till completely smooth.
- Add water, salt and garnish with 1–2 mint leaves.
- Serve chilled.

BEVERAGES

Date Smoothie

Children enjoy this smoothie as it resembles a thick chocolate shake, and tastes better, too!

Makes 1 large glass (300 ml) ■ *Prep time: 30 mins for soaking* ■ *Cook time: 5 mins*

6 dates (deseeded, chopped and soaked in ½ cup milk for 1 hour)
1½ cup milk
½ cup yogurt
1 tsp cashews, crumbled (optional)

- In a blender, add the soaked chopped dates (along with the milk) and make a fine paste. Add the rest of the milk and yogurt, and blend for 2 minutes until smooth.
- Pour into a tall beverage glass. Add crumbled cashews as a top layer. Serve chilled.

Watermelon Mocktail

Watermelon is a highly concentrated source of lycopene (an antioxidant) with wide-ranging health benefits.

Makes 1 large glass (300 ml) ■ *Prep time: 15 mins*

1 glass watermelon juice (preferably fresh)
¼ tsp cardamom powder
¼ cup crushed ice
Pinch of black salt
½ tsp *kevda* (screw-pine flower essence)
¼ cup sparkling water

- To the juice, add cardamom powder, crushed ice, *kevda*, black salt and sparkling water. Stir and serve with ice in a tall beverage glass.

Tip: Purée the watermelon, add lemon juice and serve as a sorbet. This also works as a cold soup or a dessert!

Orange Punch with Chocolate Sprinkles

A proven combo gets a new twist with this drink.

Makes 1 glass (250 ml) ■ *Prep time: 35 mins (includes time for freezing)*

½ small banana, thinly sliced
¾ glass orange juic
2 tbsp chocolate, grated (chocolate compound or any chocolate bar)
¼ cup ice cubes

- Freeze the banana slices in an airtight container for 30 minutes.
- Blend the orange juice and the sliced banana in the blender until smooth. Sprinkle grated chocolate over it and serve chilled with ice cubes.

Tip: If buying orange juice, choose one with the pulp.

Mint Amla Cooler

Amla or Indian gooseberry has valuable properties in addition to the high Vitamin C content. Very green and energizing, this drink is perfect for kids on the go.

Makes 500 ml concentrate: 15 glasses of the drink ▪ *Prep time: 25 mins*

10 medium lemons
½ cup mint leaves
¼ cup water
2½ cup brown sugar
1 tsp black salt
2 tbsp *amla* powder

- Extract the lemon juice. Blend the mint leaves in the lemon juice to a fine paste.
- Dissolve the sugar in the water. Bring to a boil to make sugar syrup.
- Add the paste to the sugar syrup and mix well. Strain through a fine sieve.
- Add black salt and *amla* powder.
- Pour the prepared concentrate into a bottle. This can be stored in the fridge for over 2 months.
- To serve the drink, add 1 part of the prepared concentrate to 3 parts of drinking water.

Tip: You could also use amla *juice (200 ml) instead of the* amla *powder.*

Coco Pina

All the goodness of fruit, milk and coconut water in one recipe! Coconut water is a great source of potassium and essential electrolytes that children need after physical activity.

Makes 1 large glass (300 ml) ■ Prep time: 10 mins

¼ cup ice cubes
¾ glass fresh coconut water
¼ glass fresh pineapple juice
¼ cup milk
2 tbsp finely chopped pineapple

- Place the ice cubes in a blender. Add pineapple juice, coconut water and milk, and blend well.
- Add the chopped pineapple and serve chilled in a tall beverage glass.

Chocomil Shake

Sweet potato, the blockbuster source of beta-carotene (an antioxidant), makes this shake creamy and nutritious.

Serves 2 ■ Prep time: 20 mins

½ cup sweet potato purée (preparation below)
1½ cups milk
2 tbsp chocolate syrup
A pinch of salt
¼ tsp nutmeg powder
1 tsp chocolate, grated

- Prepare sweet potato purée by first roasting the whole sweet potato in a moderate oven (180–200°C) for 45 minutes or boil for 10 minutes in the pressure cooker. Peel and purée the flesh in a food processor.
- Blend milk, chocolate syrup, nutmeg powder, salt and the sweet potato purée in a blender until smooth.
- Top with grated chocolate.

Snacks

Bananaraga Bread

Ragi or finger millet is considered the king of grains because it is super-rich in calcium. This is one recipe to get the kids to like this millet and reap its benefits, too.

Serves 4–6 ▪ *Prep time: 10 min–15 mins* ▪ *Cook time: 40 mins*

¼ cup ragi flour
¾ cup wholewheat flour
½ tsp baking soda
¼ tsp baking powder
½ tsp salt
½ cup brown sugar
¼ cup oil
2 egg whites
2 cups banana purée
1 tsp vanilla extract

- Spay the baking pan with oil and heat oven to 180°C.
- Mix together the dry ingredients: ragi flour, wholewheat flour, baking powder, baking soda and salt, and set aside.
- In another bowl, add sugar to the oil and mix well. To the same bowl add egg whites, banana purée and vanilla extract. To this add the flour mixture and blend well.
- Pour into a loaf/cake pan and bake for 40 minutes at 180°C–200°C. Cool before serving.

Faux Kebabs

This snack tastes like *shammi* kebabs, and at the same time, it is loaded with fibre and a host of other nutrients. These kebabs can be also used in a burger as a patty to improve the nutritive value of the otherwise 'not-so-healthy' burger.

Makes 10 medium kebabs ■ Prep time: 20 mins ■ Cook time: 15 mins

1 cup boiled black chickpea (*kala chana*)
1 onion, finely chopped
1 tsp ginger–garlic paste
½ cup mashed potatoes
Salt to taste
3 tsp oil for pan-frying

- Mash the boiled chickpea in a blender till it resembles kneaded dough.
- Add chopped onions and the ginger–garlic paste, mashed potatoes and salt to the *chana* dough.
- Mix well and divide the dough into 10 portions. Shape each portion into small discs.
- Heat oil in a pan and cook the patties in the oil until brown. Serve with any fresh chutney.

Note: Instead of potatoes, boiled rice could be used as an alternative binder.

Quick Quesadilla

Although quesadilla is a Mexican dish, this Indian version works just as well. Try it with leftover rotis.

Serves 4 ■ Prep time: 20 mins ■ Cook time: 10 mins

For the shell
2 rotis (any flour – barley/ wholewheat/multigrain
1 tsp oil/butter

For tomato paste
2 medium tomatoes, chopped
5 cloves garlic, chopped
1 medium onion, chopped
Pinch of mace (*javitri*)
Salt to taste
¼ tsp sugar
½ tsp oil

For the filling
2 cloves garlic, finely chopped
1 medium onion, chopped
1 cup red and green capsicum, chopped
½ tsp butter/oil
½ tsp chilli powder
½ tsp coriander powder

- To prepare the tomato paste, heat oil in a wok, add chopped garlic, onions and sauté for a minute. Add chopped tomatoes and cook until soft and paste-like. Add salt, spices and sugar.
- Prepare the filling by heating oil/butter in a pan, toss in the garlic, onion and the capsicum. Cook uncovered for 1 minute. Add salt, coriander and chilli powder.
- On the face of the chapatti, spread a layer of tomato paste and top it evenly with the sautéed veggies. Cover with the second roti and press gently all around as with a sandwich.

- Place on a *tawa* and cook on both sides till slightly brown.
- Remove from the *tawa*, and cut into sections or wedges, like a pizza. Serve hot.

Tip: Add cottage cheese/processed cheese to the veggies to enhance the taste of the dish. The process of cooking on the tawa *can be replaced by baking the roti sandwich in the oven for 5 minutes.*

Pretty Perfect Pancakes

It is possible to whip up a healthy, tasty pancake without using any refined flour! After tasting these, my kids refused to eat the usual refined flour pancakes – adequate endorsement for its acceptability!

Makes 6 medium ▪ Prep time: 1 hour ▪ Cook time: 10 mins

1 ½ cup oats	1 tsp baking powder
2 cups milk	2 tsp brown sugar
5 tbsp wholewheat flour	2 tsp butter

- In a pan, soak oats in milk and leave aside for an hour.
- To this, add wholewheat flour, baking powder and sugar, and mix well.
- Add butter to a skillet and heat.
- Pour approximately one ladle full of the mixture and spread in the shape of a pancake. Cover and cook for 2 minutes or so. Turn over and cook the other side, too, until slightly brown.
- Serve with slices of any seasonal fruit and honey.

Triple-S Sticks

This snack can be pan-fried or deep-fried depending on the occasion. The spinach, sesame and soya paneer included in the recipe are all great sources of nutrients.

Makes 10–12 sticks ■ Prep time: 25 mins ■ Cook time: 15 mins

250g/1 cup soya paneer (tofu), grated
½ cup thick spinach purée
Salt to taste
1 tbsp cornflour
2 tbsp sesame seed powder
1 cup breadcrumbs (from wholewheat bread)
1 tbsp oil for pan-frying/deep-frying

- Mash the tofu in a bowl. Add the spinach purée, salt and cornflour to it and mix well. Knead well and place in the freezer for 20 minutes.
- Prepare the coating by adding the sesame seed powder to the breadcrumbs.
- Take the dough out of the freezer and give it the desired shape, such as sticks/nuggets. Roll the sticks/nuggets in the breadcrumb mixture well.
- In a frying pan, add 1 tbsp oil and heat. Place the soya sticks/nuggets in the pan and allow to cook until they turn brown. Cook the other side until brown.
- Serve with any chutney or ketchup.

***Tip:** You can substitute tofu with cottage cheese or mozzarella cheese, too! Similarly, substitute spinach with any vegetable of your choice.*

Choco Waffle Surprise

Did you know that it is possible to make delicious waffles without using refined flour? Here is one way to do it.

Makes 4 waffles ■ Prep time: 10 mins ■ Cook time: 6–7 mins

4 eggs
8 tbsp milk
2 tbsp sugar
½ cup almond powder
½ cup amaranth (*cholai*) flour/rice flour
2 tbsp cocoa powder
2 tbsp butter/coconut oil

- Blend eggs and milk with a beater. Add cocoa, almond powder and amaranth, and blend gently.
- Add butter (slightly melted) or oil and mix well.
- Pour into a greased waffle maker. When done in 6–7 minutes, remove and serve with honey.

Tip: Make the waffles following the method described. Extra waffles can be stored in the freezer in an airtight freezer-safe bag. Remember to cool the waffles before you put them into the freezer bag. Take the waffles out of the bag as and when required, pop into a toaster and they are ready to be served.

Hearty Cutlet

Yes, you can go by the name – it's more than likely to win everyone's heart. It won my heart because in this one dish you get to eat the right combo of cereal/legume and veggies.

Makes 12 pieces ■ Prep time: 20 mins ■ Cook time: 10 mins

½ cup *moong* dal (*dhuli*)
½ cup oats
2 tbsp yogurt
3 tbsp onion, finely chopped
½ green chilli, chopped
2 tsp *chaat* masala
½ tsp turmeric powder
1 tsp ginger–garlic paste
2 tbsp chopped leaves (coriander/radish/ fenugreek)
1 tsp lemon juice
1 tbsp cooking oil

- Boil the dal in 1 cup water for 10 minutes. If the dal is too watery, cook until it becomes thick.
- Add all the ingredients mentioned above except oats.
- Roast the oats in a skillet/*karahi* without any oil so as to slightly toast them. Add to the dal mixture.
- Divide into 12 portions and shape as you like.
- Place the cutlets in a greased pan and fry until they turn light brown on one side; then turn over and cook until they are lightly browned on the other side, too.
- Serve with a salad.

Methi Mathri Chaat

This dish is a deal breaker when your kids are fussing about food. It is flavourful and filling.

Serves 4 ■ Prep time: 30 mins ■ Cook time: 20 mins

For the mathri
½ cup wheat flour
½ cup carrot leaves
¼ tsp cumin powder
¼ tsp coriander powder
1tsp *kasoori methi* (dried fenugreek)
2 tsp oil

For yogurt dressing
1 cup yogurt
½ tsp cumin powder
½ tsp *chaat* masala
½ tsp black salt
2 tbsp *imli* chutney

- Measure out the above-mentioned ingredients for the *mathri* (except oil) and knead into a stiff dough with ½ cup water. Leave the dough covered for 30 mins.
- Grease a baking tray with a thin layer of oil.
- Divide the dough into 4 portions and roll out each portion into a thin circular shape with the help of a rolling pin.
- With a biscuit cutter, cut the thinly rolled sheet into small circles. Prick the surface of the dough with a fork. Place on a lightly greased baking tray and place it in a preheated oven (to 180°C). Bake for 5 minutes on each side.
- Cool. To serve, break each *mathri* into half, put it in a bowl and sprinkle sprouts over it.
- Mix all the ingredients for the yogurt dressing and spoon out on the *mathri*–sprouts preparation.
- The healthy, wholesome *chaat* is ready to serve.

Fruit Kebab

There couldn't be an easier way to include fruits into your child's diet. Vary the fruits according to the season and get the benefit of the available fruit colours.

Serves 4 ■ Prep time: 1 hour (soaking) + 15 mins

- 8 cubes of watermelon
- 8 cubes of muskmelon
- 8 cubes of pineapple
- 8 grapes/strawberry
- 8 bamboo skewers (soaked in water for 1 hour)/ toothpicks
- 1 tbsp honey
- 1 tbsp walnuts, coarsely ground

- Thread each skewer with one piece of each fruit one after the other, until the skewer is covered.
- At the tip of the skewer, place a grape or strawberry. Serve with a dip, or with honey blended with ground walnuts.

***Tip:** Alternately, the skewer can be placed in the oven for 10 minutes until the fruit sugar caramelizes.*

Chaat in a Cone

Use the good old papad to prepare the cone and fill it with the goodness of beans.

Serves 4 ■ Prep time: 15 mins ■ Cook time: 5 mins

For the cone
4 dal papads, each divided into half

For the filling
1 cup black-eyed beans, boiled
1½ tbsp cooking oil
1 tsp chopped garlic
1 medium tomato, chopped
1 small capsicum, sliced into thin strips
1 medium onion, chopped
1 tbsp chopped coriander
1 tbsp thick tamarind (*imli*) extract
1 tsp salt

- In a frying pan, heat oil and add garlic and onion. Cook until onions turn translucent.
- Add the chopped tomatoes followed by the boiled beans and capsicum.
- Stir well and add the tamarind extract.
- Add salt and chopped coriander leaves. The filling for the cone is ready.
- Roast the papad halves by rolling a half like a cone and holding it over the flame with a pair of tongs.
- Add a tablespoon of the filling into each cone and serve.

Tip: You could select the variety of beans according to your child's preference.

Lunch Box

Healthy Samosa

Tasty finger food that's also great as a lunch option for kids. This healthy samosa recipe does not leave you feeling guilty when the kids eat it.

Serves 6 ■ Prep time: 20 mins ■ Cook time: 10 mins

For the shell
¼ cup rice flour
¼ cup *urad* dal flour
Hot water
¼ tsp salt

For the filling
½ cup peas (frozen or fresh)
¼ cup paneer, crumbled
½ cumin powder
½ tsp green chillies (optional)
1 tsp coriander leaves, chopped
Salt to taste

- Thaw the peas, if frozen, and remove excess water.
- Heat ½ tsp oil in a wok, add peas and cook for 2–3 minutes. Add spices and coriander leaves and cook for another minute.
- Mix rice flour and *urad* dal flour in a separate bowl. Add salt and knead to form a stiff dough with hot water. Keep aside for 20 minutes, covered with a damp cloth.
- Divide the dough into small pellets. Roll out like mini thin puris. Divide into half using a knife. Form a cone and fill in the peas and crumbled paneer.
- Deep-fry till light brown.
- Drain the excess oil and serve with mint chutney.

***Tip:** Add 1 tbsp* suji *to the rice–dal flour when kneading, to make the cover crispy.*

Wow Wrap

Wraps are the current favourite with children. Make them at home almost effortlessly and wait till you get requests from all your child's friends for more!

Makes 2 wraps ■ Prep time: 15 mins ■ Cook time: 7 mins

½ cup tofu or cottage cheese (mashed)
½ cup spring onions
¼ cup coriander leaves
1 tsp garlic, minced
1 tsp honey
1 tsp vinegar
Salt to taste
1 tbsp sesame oil
2 chapattis (made from any healthy flour)

- Mix the tofu and all the listed ingredients together (excluding chapattis).
- Spread a thick layer of the mixture over one surface of the chapatti and fold the chapatti into half.
- Place the folded chapattis into a sandwich maker and cook for 5–7 minutes or until slightly brown.
- Serve hot with chutney/ketchup.

Tip: The chapattis could also be made with spinach or beetroot purée (as explained in the Tricolour Paratha recipe). This will add to the appeal and increase the nutritional worth, too.

Yum Yam Kebab

So yummy, your kids will never guess what these are made of! Contrary to the widely held belief, yam is a great source of carbohydrate, soluble fibre and potassium.

Serves 4 ■ Prep time: 20 mins ■ Cook time: 10 mins

2 cups yam purée (preparation below)
1 onion, sliced and cooked till brown
1 tbsp chopped coriander leaves
½ tsp cumin powder
½ tsp coriander powder
½ tsp garam masala
2 tbsp lemon juice
1 tsp ginger-garlic paste
½ cup roasted *chana* powder
3 tbsp oil

- Prepare the yam purée by boiling the yam in the pressure cooker for 10 minutes, removing the peel and mashing the pulp into a smooth paste.
- Mix all the spices – cumin powder, coriander powder and garam masala – together.
- In a grinder, mix together browned onions, fresh coriander leaves, the spices, ginger–garlic paste and lemon juice. Add this paste to the mashed yam pulp.
- Add the roasted *chana* powder to the yam–spices mixture. Once added, the mixture acquires the consistency of chapatti dough.
- Make the desired shape with this dough by dividing it into small portions.
- Heat the oil on the *tawa* and shallow fry the kebabs.
- Serve with chutney (made from raw mango, garlic and jaggery).

No-Bake Pizza

This home-made pizza is nutritious and tasty – and to top it all, it needs no baking!

Makes 12–15 mini pizzas ■ Prep time: 20 mins ■ Cook time: 20 mins

For base

½ cup wheat flour
1½ cup oats/amaranth seeds
½ cup powdered almonds
½ to 1 cup carrots and cauliflower, crumbled in the food processor
Salt and pepper to taste
1 tsp oregano powder
2 eggs, beaten

For the topping

5 medium tomatoes
10–15 basil leaves
¼ cup (1 small bunch) of leaves (spinach salad rocket any other)
½ cup shredded cheese (mozzarella/Cheddar)
2 tbsp olive oil

- In a mixing bowl, bring together flour, oats/amaranth seeds, almond powder, crumbled vegetables, salt, pepper and oregano, and mix well. Make a well in the centre.
- Beat the eggs and add to the centre of the prepared mix. Mix well. The dough should be soft and moist.
- Divide the dough into 12–15 portions and make small thin discs like a mini pizza base.
- Cook the discs on both sides on a *tawa* without an oil.
- Blend the tomatoes and basil leaves in the blender. Add salt, pepper and olive oil. Spoon the tomato–basil mixture on to the small discs.
- Top with chicken/mushrooms/veggies if desired.

- Grate cheese and sprinkle on top. Drizzle oil over it.

Tip: Alternatively, place the discs in the OTG for 5-10 minutes so as to melt the cheese slightly and cook the base. This is the baked version of the same healthy pizza.

Best Bean Burger

A great dish for all those kids who don't like vegetarian burgers. They get the benefit of beans without even knowing it.

Makes 8 patties for 8 burgers ■ Prep time: 10 mins ■ Cook time: 15 mins

2 cups kidney beans (*rajma*), boiled
1 tsp garlic paste
1 tsp ginger paste
½ tsp green chillies
1 tsp coriander leaves, chopped
Salt to taste
6 tbsp breadcrumbs
4 tsp oil
8 burger buns
1 cheese slice
Round slices of onion and tomato

- Mash the boiled kidney beans just enough to flatten them enough to make a patty shape. Add the ginger, garlic, chillies, coriander and salt, and mix well.
- Coat the patty completely with breadcrumbs.
- In a pan, spray cooking oil and cook the patty on both sides over medium heat. Place 1 patty in a burger bun along with tomato slices, onion slices, a cheese slice and ketchup, and serve.

Funky Cutlets

These cutlets with a difference are irresistible when it comes to those hungry times.

Serves 2 ■ Prep time: 30 mins ■ Cook time: 20 mins

1 cup paneer, crumbled (preferably made at home)
Salt to taste
½ cup mixed vegetable purée
1 tbsp cornflour
1 tbsp flaxseed powder
1 cup amaranth seeds (*ramdana*), coarsely ground
1 tbsp oil

- In a bowl, mix together the crumbled paneer, salt, vegetable purée and cornflour. Divide into 6–8 portions and give it any interesting shape.
- In another bowl, mix together *ramdana* flour and flaxseed powder.
- Roll the paneer portions in the flaxseed and amaranth mixture and place in the fridge for 20 minutes.
- Add oil in a pan and cook the chilled paneer cutlets on medium heat, turning them over so that they are evenly cooked.
- Serve with dip/chutney.

***Tip:** Replace the crumbled paneer with paneer slices/cubes, if you like.*

Dips and Sauces

Healthy Mayo

This recipe does not require raw eggs as in the conventional mayonnaise recipe. Raw eggs carry health risks and are best avoided.

Makes 1 cup ■ Prep time: 20 mins

1 cup low-fat milk
1 tsp sorghum (jowar) flour
1 tsp lemon juice
½ tsp sugar
¼ tsp salt
¼ tsp pepper
½ tsp mustard powder
½ cup oil (peanut/olive/sesame)
1 tbsp vinegar

- Add milk to the sorghum flour gradually so that no lumps are formed. Cook over low heat in a pan until slightly thick.
- In a blender, add mustard powder, salt, lemon juice, sugar and pepper. Pour into the thickened milk.
- Add oil and vinegar alternately in small amounts into the thickened milk. Run the blender each time the oil/vinegar is poured in.
- The healthy mayo is ready. It can be used as a dip or as a substitute for butter in sandwiches.

***Tip:** You could choose from a range of healthy flours and replace sorghum with any of them.*

Blushing Dip

This is an effective way to get kids to eat beetroot, which has some remarkable properties that keep blood pressure under control – both yours and your kid's!

Makes 2 cups ■ Prep time: 10 mins ■ Cook time: 15 mins

200g beetroot (boiled with skin)
25g yogurt (thick)
2 tbsp vinegar
1 tbsp lemon juice
1 tsp salt
½ tsp sugar
½ tsp cumin powder
1 tsp crushed nuts

- Boil the beetroot with skin in the minimum quantity of water required for approximately 10 minutes. Drain the excess water.
- Peel the boiled beetroot and put it a food processor to make a smooth paste.
- Add vinegar, salt and sugar to it and mix well.
- Add cumin powder, mix and pour into a bowl. Add yogurt, lemon juice and nuts.
- Serve as a dip with potatoes, meat or breads.

Greek Dip

The not-so-healthy foods, like potato chips, which kids do eat once in a while can be supplemented with this dip to improve the overall nutrition profile.

Makes 1 cup ■ Prep time: 15 mins

¾ cup chickpea (boiled and made into a paste)
2 tbsp grated cheese
1 tbsp lemon juice
2 cloves garlic, finely crushed or chopped
Salt to taste
¼ tsp chilli powder
¼ tsp pepper
⅛ tsp onion powder

- To the chickpea paste, add the other ingredients and blend well. Serve with toasted bread or chips.

Red Chutney

This fiery-looking chutney goes well with Neer Dosa, *upma* and cutlets.

Makes 1 cup ■ Prep time: 5 mins ■ Cook time: 12 mins

½ tsp oil
1 onion, chopped
1 tomato, chopped
A pinch asafoetida
A few curry leaves

- In a wok, heat ½ tsp oil, add chopped onions and brown slightly.
- Add chopped tomatoes and cook for 3–4 minutes till soft.
- Purée the onion and tomato in a food processor.
- Pour out into serving dish.
- In a pan with a drop of oil, add asafoetida and curry leaves. Cook and add to the ground tomato–onion paste. The chutney is ready.

Romesco Sauce

This one looks rich like mayonnaise but is really light on the palate.

Makes 1 cup ■ Prep time: 20 mins

1 medium red bell pepper
½ cup olive oil
½ cup cashews
5–6 cloves garlic, chopped
4 medium tomatoes
2 tsp vinegar
¾ tsp salt

- Split the bell pepper by dividing it longitudinally into two sections. Place it in the oven rack and grill for 20 minutes on high heat. This provides the smoked flavour to the dish. Or you could roast the pepper by holding it with a pair of tongs over the stove flame for 5 minutes, rotating it all over.
- In the meantime, blanch the tomatoes by dipping them in boiling water for 2 to 3 minutes. Remove from water, peel and keep aside.
- Take olive oil in a pan and warm slightly. Add cashews, garlic, the smoked pepper and tomato pulp. Put the mixture into a food processor and purée until smooth.
- Add vinegar and salt.
- Serve this sauce with veggies, chicken or mix it into pasta. Store in an airtight container in the fridge for 3–4 days.

Tip: You could use blanched, peeled almonds instead of cashews as most original recipes suggest. If you prefer a richer feel, add a shredded slice of bread to the sauce while puréeing it.

Cooking for Fun (DIY for Kids)

A combination of three healthy foods – fruits, yogurt and nuts – makes for such a palatable dish!

Fruit Pops

Makes 4–6 popsicles. ■ Prep time: 15 mins ■ Freezing time: 1 hour

2 cups mango purée/strawberries/cherries, pitted
2 cups yogurt
1 tbsp roasted watermelon seeds/chia seeds
½ cup sugar

- Blend all the ingredients (except the seeds) in a blender/food processor until smooth.
- Add the seeds to the blended mixture.
- Pour into *kulfi*/popsicle moulds.
- Freeze and serve as a dessert.

***Tip:** Chopped nuts may be used instead of seeds.*

Potato Boats

A little bit of tweaking makes these healthy potatoes tasty.

Makes 4 portions ■ Prep time: 15 mins

4–5 medium boiled potatoes, peeled
½ medium onion, chopped finely
¼ red capsicum, chopped finely
1 tsp raw mustard oil
1 tsp coriander leaves, chopped
½ tsp mustard powder
½ tsp pepper powder

- Slit each boiled potato lengthwise and scoop out a small portion in the centre so that a thick shell remains. Reserve the scooped out potato.
- To this reserved scooped potato, add onions, capsicum, mustard oil, coriander leaves and spices. Mix well and stuff back into the potato shell.
- Serve as a snack.

***Tip:** This recipe can be replicated with cucumbers as well. Follow this process:*

Peel cucumber and slit into half lengthwise. Scoop out the seeds from the centre with a teaspoon. Make a wide and deep hollow without damaging the shell. Fill in the scooped-out portion with either Greek Dip (see recipe) or the potato-mustard filling prepared above.

Super Strong Salad

Colours and crunch – this salad has both!

Serves 4 ■ Prep time: 15 mins

2 cups grated carrot
1 medium cucumber, cut into ¼ inch thick discs
4 tbsp peanuts, crushed
2 tsp oil (sesame/peanut)
1 tbsp lemon juice
1 tsp vinegar
2 green chillies, made into a paste
2 pieces of lemongrass, shredded

- Combine all the above ingredients and serve with meals, as a snack, or on the side with soup.

Tip: Use balsamic vinegar or apple cider vinegar for added flavour.

One Potato Two Potato

Baking potato wedges instead of frying them makes them instantly healthy and guilt-free!

Serves 2 ■ *Prep time: 10 mins* ■ *Cook time: 30–40 mins*

5 medium potatoes (500g)
1 tbsp oil
1 tsp garlic paste
2 tbsp onion paste
½ tsp salt
¼ tsp pepper
½ tsp oregano (optional)

- Peel and slice the potatoes into wedges. The thickness of the wedges should not be more than ½ inch. Place in a bowl.
- Mix together the onion paste, garlic paste and the seasoning (salt, pepper and oregano).
- Rub the prepared paste over the potato wedges so that all the wedges are evenly coated.
- Heat oven to 200–250°C. Spread an aluminium sheet over the baking tray or coat the baking tray with cooking oil.
- Arrange the potatoes over the tray/aluminium foil and bake until evenly brown (approx. 30 minutes).
- Serve hot.

Mintnut Sandwich

Crunchy, munchy and so healthy, this snack will prove to be a saviour in those 'I'm-so-hungry' moments.

Serves 2 ■ Prep time: 15 mins

2 slices bread (wholegrain)
2 tbsp peanuts, roasted and ground coarsely
1 tsp mint leaves, chopped
1 tsp mint/coriander leaves, chopped
A pinch of salt

For garlic butter

1 tsp butter
1 garlic clove
¼ tsp oregano/chilli flakes

- Prepare garlic butter by adding 1 clove crushed garlic to 1 tsp butter. Add a pinch of either oregano flakes or chilli flakes and mix together.
- Make a paste of mint and coriander leaves (in the blender) with a pinch of salt and add to the prepared garlic butter.
- Add the peanuts and mix well.
- On one side of a bread slice, apply this paste and cover with the other slice. Cut into any desired shape and serve.

Lemony Mushrooms

White button mushrooms are a great source of Vitamin D, digestive enzymes and B vitamins.

Serves 4 ■ *Prep time: 10 mins* ■ *Cook time: 10 mins*

500g white button mushrooms
2 tsp butter
1 tsp salt
1 tsp pepper, freshly crushed
2 tsp lemon juice
2 tsp dried parsley or fresh leaves

- Wash mushrooms and wipe them dry with a piece of absorbent cloth. Slice them thinly.
- Heat the butter in a pan and then add the mushrooms.
- Sprinkle salt, pepper, lemon juice and dried parsley.
- Cover and cook for 10 minutes.
- Serve on toast or with rice.

Garlic-Basil Bruschetta

Here's adding more nutrition to a kids' favourite!

Makes 4 portions ■ *Cook time: 5 mins*

4 slices of bread
2 tsp butter
4 cloves garlic
1 tsp chopped basil leaves
Oregano and chilli flakes to taste
1 small tomato

- Soften the butter and add crushed garlic to it. Blend well. Add chopped basil leaves and mix well.
- Toast the bread in the toaster/grill or on a *tawa*.
- Spread a layer of garlic–basil butter and sprinkle chilli flakes/oregano flakes while the toast is still hot. Serve with a slice of tomato.

Yoyo Yogurt

Kids usually don't like to eat plain yogurt. Try this innovative version with the goodness of almonds and greens.

Serves 4 ■ Prep time: 15 mins

2 cups curd (thick)
¾ tsp garlic, chopped finely
3 tbsp almond, sliced
2 tbsp radish leaves, chopped
1 tsp oil (olive preferred)
Black salt to taste
Mint leaves to garnish

- Blend the curd well to make a smooth paste. Add the rest of the ingredients including mint and almonds. Serve chilled as part of main meal or as a dip with snacks.

Maha Munchies

Ditch the readymade namkeens and make your own signature version this way.

Serves 4 ■ Cook time: 10 mins

1 cup foxnuts (*makhana*)
1 cup popcorn (popped and unsalted)
½ cup raisins
1 tsp oil
½ tsp salt
1 tsp cumin powder
1 tsp black pepper powder

- Heat oil in a wok and add the foxnuts to it.
- Roast the nuts gently, stirring over a low flame.
- When slightly brown, add the popcorn and raisins to the wok.
- Add the spices and salt, and continue to cook for another 2 minutes.
- Remove from fire and serve the warm, healthy *namkeen*.

SECTION 8
TIPS AND TRICKS

[20]

101 TIPS

Baby Steps Lead to a Big Impact

1 Foods other than breast milk should not be introduced in a child's diet before the age of 4–6 months.

2 Rice in the form of gruel or *khichdi* is the grain of choice as the baby's first food.

3 Mashed banana, puréed apples and sweet potato are other choices as first weaning options to solid food.

4 Introduce one new food at a time with a gap of no less than three days.

5 It may take even up to 10–20 trials of a new food for your baby to accept it – don't give up before that! Be patient.

6 Added salt and sugar is not required in baby foods. Mild spices and herbs are fine.

7 Juices should not replace milk in a child's diet.

8 Excess juice consumption could lead to diarrhoea.

9 Honey should not be added to a child's diet before 12 months of age.

10 Healthy infants on breast milk require no supplemental water except in hot weather.

11 Hard round foods such as nuts, candies, popcorn, raw carrots and grapes, are best avoided in children younger than 2 years as there is a risk of choking. Children in this age group to be supervised while eating.

12 Do not use the microwave to heat milk for children. 'Hot spots' develop due to uneven heating that occurs.

13 Do not introduce cow's milk to the child's diet before the age of 12 months.

14 Do not share spoons and forks with kids. The saliva and microbes from the adult's mouth could predispose kids to dental caries.

Milk and Dairy Do's

15 Milk products vary widely in their fat content, so choose wisely. What you choose will make a big difference to the fat and saturated fat content of your child's diet.

16 Adding water to milk does not reduce its fat content. It only dilutes the nutrients.

17 Frozen yogurt, unlike fresh yogurt, lacks the live bacteria that are beneficial.

Protein Truths

18 Soya protein is the only complete vegetable protein as it has all the amino acids that we require. The rest of the vegetable protein foods need to be eaten in combination with other foods to match the complete protein profile.

19 Amino acids (the building blocks of proteins) can get wasted if enough energy (calories) is not present in the diet.

20 Digestibility of proteins varies from food to food. In general, proteins from meats and eggs top the list. They are most easily digested and absorbed. Soya and legumes follow with 80–90 per cent digestibility.

21 Insufficient protein intake in children can make them susceptible to infections, so make sure to give them the appropriate amount of proteins through the day.

22 If you cook proteins in moist heat (with water), as opposed to dry-heat methods such a frying, grilling and broiling, it makes them easier to digest.

Fruits and Juices

23 Beware of the words 'Fruit Drink' on the label: it is likely to have negligible fruit pulp and more sugar and artificial flavours.

24 With the exception of avocado, fruits do not contain any fat.

25 No more than one-third of the fruit allowance for children should be in the form of juice.

Veggies

26 Foods with the most nutrients per calorie are veggies – particularly carrots, tomatoes, capsicum, mushrooms, beetroot and the leafy variety.

27 Do not use cooking soda while boiling or steaming veggies as it destroys the B vitamins in the food.

28 When boiling veggies, first boil the water, then add the veggies to the boiling water.

29 Overcooking veggies reduces the levels of folic acid present in them.

30 Spinach has a lower calcium content compared to other leafy vegetables such as mint, coriander, fenugreek, beet greens and lettuce. Never discard edible leaves!

31 Lemon peels have great nutritional worth. Do not throw them away. Grate the peel and add to drinking water, salads and water for ice cubes.

32 Always choose red/deep pink and yellow onions instead of the white ones. The latter have fewer antioxidants.

33 Select the darkest green leafy vegetables for their higher antioxidant value.

34 In 1 litre of warm water, add ¼ cup vinegar and 4 tsp (2%) salt. Soak vegetables and fruits in it for 30 minutes. Rinse off with drinking water. Doing this reduces the pesticide residues considerably.

35 Plant foods contain no cholesterol. This includes peanuts, walnuts and cashewnuts.

Fibre

36 To determine how much fibre a child needs, you could add 5 to the child's age and arrive at the figure. A 6-year-old child needs 11g fibre per day. This formula works for those between 3 to 19 years of age.

37 Insoluble fibre prevents constipation and encourages the growth of friendly bacteria in the intestines. The main sources are minimally processed grains, edible peels of fruit and vegetables, and seeds and nuts.

38 Soluble fibre is important for maintaining blood sugar levels, lowering cholesterol and controlling hunger pangs. You can get it from fruits, vegetables, peas, oats, soya and dals.

39 Genrally speaking, the rougher and coarser the food, the fewer calories it provides.

Fat Facts

40 Store oils/fats in a cool, dark place. The best place for them is the refrigerator.

41 Oil/fat used for frying should be strained after use so as to remove all crumbs of food from it. Such particles accelerate spoilage. The strained oil can be used again only for cooking but not for frying.

42 A low-fat diet is not necessarily a low-calorie one. A low-fat diet could be high in refined carbohydrates and sugars – and that's just as bad.

43 A label which is marked 'cholesterol free' may not contain cholesterol but may be loaded with other harmful ingredients. A *namkeen* fried in *vanaspati* (hydrogenated vegetable oil) does not contain cholesterol but has harmful trans fats.

44 It's not just the quantity but also the quality of fat that affects health profoundly. This is why certain high-fat foods *can* be part of a healthy diet.

45 People mistakenly believe that eating fat-free foods will ensure weight reduction. However, other foods taken in excess can also be fattening.

46 The oil that withstands the effect of heat best is coconut oil. Thus, this is the one that can be used for baking and frying.

47 Margarine is not always better than butter. Check the ingredient list: if the margarine contains hydrogenated fats, avoid it.

48 One need not eat fat in every meal of the day, but we do need a source of carbohydrate at regular intervals. Our liver can store only a day's

supply of carbs, which is why we need a steady supply of them.

49 Olive oil is not the only oil that provides health benefits. Other healthy oils are sesame, rice bran, mustard, canola and peanut. Such oils also contain a good mix of fatty acids that the body requires.

50 Even healthy oils such as olive oil can cause harm if consumed in excess.

51 'Light olive oil' is not light in terms of calories, but 'light' refers to its colour.

52 Among the many commonly used cooking oils, mustard and soya are those that contain reasonable amounts of omega-3 fats.

53 Always go for unrefined, cold-pressed oils over the refined oils. Refining is done only to benefit the manufacturers.

General Cooking and Eating

54 Eggs can be substituted with 2 tbsp of yogurt when making cakes or muffins. Another replacement for eggs that works well is 1 teaspoon of baking powder in lieu of 1 egg.

55 Do not add tomatoes or *imli* too early when cooking lentils. This makes them difficult to cook and chewy.

56 Bread recipes require usually about 1 tsp of salt per loaf. If one is watching out for salt, keep this in mind.

57 For easy peeling, immerse garlic cloves in boiling water for 5 seconds.

58 To get rid of excessive salt from soups, add egg white to it while cooking. The egg white absorbs salt on the surface and settles at the bottom, from where you can remove it.

59 Do not discard the leftover whey when you make cottage cheese. Add this to gravies or knead it into the dough for making bread/chappattis.

60 When you add oats to boiling water, you will get a coarse texture. If you add oats to room-temperature water and then cook, you will get a creamier texture.

Eating Habits

61 If a child is thin, it does not mean s/he should be allowed to eat unhealthy.

63 If your child refuses to eat the food being served, simply remove it after 30 minutes (without a fight/comments). Do not cook another meal to replace it. Instead, offer a healthy snack an hour and a half later.

62 Using a straw for drinking will reduce bloating and gas that children often complain about.

64 The larger the container, the more we tend to eat or drink. That's why small plates and glasses are advocated when weight loss is desired.

65 If you want to be mentally alert and energetic, ditch fat-laden large-volume meals (for e.g., pulao with *dum aloo*).

66 Hot liquids tend to make you feel fuller and and, therefore, less hungry. They make for a good choice if you want to cut down food intake.

67 Paneer, potatoes and *rajma* cannot serve as a substitute for vegetables.

68 Consuming raw eggs is not a good idea for many reasons. The B vitamin biotin and iron both get released when you cook eggs. Raw eggs carry the risk of Salmonella infection.

69 The larger the container (plates/glasses), the more we tend to consume.

70 All sour foods are not necessarily rich in Vitamin C. Tamarind is low in Vitamin C while lemon is high on this vitamin.

71 Caffeine is present not just in tea and coffee but also in chocolates and aerated drinks.

72 All fad diets ask you to give up one or more food groups – that's a sign to be wary of.

Food as Medicine

73 Trying to clear congestion? Go for hot salsa or chicken soup rather than cough drops.

74 Boil water with 3 cloves of garlic, a clove (*laung*) and 1 cinnamon stick. Use this water for steam inhalation. It helps clear up respiratory passages.

75 Mixing equal parts of onion juice and water makes an effective remedy for diarrhoea. Drink it up!

76 Chewing on a piece of ginger cures nausea and loss of appetite.

77 Raw garlic has very potent antibiotic properties. Crush 2–3 garlic cloves and add to chutney or salad.

78 Honey is as effective in soothing the throat and supressing a cough as many cough medicines.

Meats

79 The breast of the chicken has the lowest fat and calorie content among all its parts.

80 If you have to cook poultry that is not a young bird, use moist heat, i.e., water or other liquid and simmer.

81 Lowering the pH of meats (adding lemon or curd) while cooking, improves its taste.

82 Avoid cooking fish on high heat as this will make it tough. While steaming fish, add a little lemon juice; this keeps the flesh white.

83 Shellfish (lobster, crab and shrimp) should be dipped in simmering salt water very briefly as a first step when cooking it. This will help retain the juiciness and tenderness.

Sweet Tips

84 Chocolate is derived from cacao beans, which contain small amounts of caffeine and theobromine. Eating too many chocolates late at night can keep you awake!

85 Heat augments sweetness; that's why a gulab jamun served hot will taste sweeter than the cold version. Adding less sugar to desserts that are served hot works well.

86 There are certain spices that enhance sweetness, such as cloves, cinnamon and nutmeg.

87 A tiny pinch of salt can make food taste sweeter. This is the reason a little salt is added to most desserts and cake recipes.

88 Sugar cravings do not occur due to a deficiency of sugar. Go for a protein-rich food and it will help control the craving.

89 The calorie count of brown sugar and white sugar is the same. The only difference is that brown sugar has some minerals present in it.

Breads and More

90 Brown bread can be made with any kind of flour, including white flour. The colour of bread could be from the molasses used in it.

91 Rice is digested faster than chapattis because of the lower fibre content. This is why one feels hungry sooner after eating an all-rice meal.

92 Eating too much starch (bread/rice/pasta) on an empty stomach will make you sleepy.

93 Mixing carbohydrates and proteins in a meal is not harmful as it is made out to be in some fad diet plans. Most food items contain a combinations of carbs and proteins, and total exclusion of one from the other is not possible.

94 The best way to cook brown rice is to boil 3 cups water, add 1 cup rice to it, let it boil uncovered for 5 minutes. Then reduce heat and simmer. Cover with a lid, leaving a small gap. This rice takes 20 minutes to cook.

95 Don't be bogged down by counting calories minutely. The simple way to get it right is to choose whole grains over refined ones.

Yet Some More

96 It is possible for a vegetarian meal to be unhealthy (e.g., fried potatoes, refined flour puris, high-fat paneer) and a non-vegetarian meal to be healthy (lean cuts of meat in small amounts along with fibre-rich cereal and a variety of vegetables).

97 Many minerals dissolved in water are actually desirable for good health. The RO system

eliminates most of the minerals. Do not go for the RO system unless the TDS (Total Dissolved Solids) levels are very high.

98 Almond milk is easy to make: Take 1½ cup almonds, ¾ cup water and 1 tsp vanilla extract. Blend well, strain and serve.

99 Corn or maize is a healthy grain. One can include corn in appropriate portions as a substitute for many of the refined cereal snacks. Omit the extra butter when making popcorn.

100 A balanced diet with an occasional treat is the practical approach to healthy eating. It allows for eating for pleasure as well as good health. The 80:20 rule works well for most teenagers, which means they stick to a healthy diet 80 per cent of the time, and 20 per cent of the time, they could indulge within limits.

101 The fat but active child needs dietary modifications. The thin, inactive one needs to build physical activity into his/her life. Being physically active in the teens lowers the chances of a heart attack later in life. Eventually, both weight and fitness matter.

Acknowledgements

It is only after writing this book that I realise how very indispensable these acknowledgements are! There are so many people to thank, and I am not sure if I'd be able to thank them enough.

I'd like to thank Dr Deepak Chopra, the world-renowned wellness guru, who took out time despite his extremely busy schedule to take a look at what I had written.

Dr Anupam Sibal sets the stage for this book with the most befitting foreword. A distinguished paediatrician, well-versed with the problems that parents face today, Dr Sibal encouraged me to take on this project for the sake of the health of the future generations.

I would never have written this book had it not been for my long-standing friend, Dr Purnima Gupta. She has been a constant source of strength and support throughout the writing period. She never failed to be my sounding board and coaxed me into writing, with such persistence that I had no choice but to write.

This book would not have seen the light of day without the help of my dear friend, Professor Anu Kapur. Being a prolific writer and an astute academic, she made for a wonderful mentor.

She has invested tremendous effort in providing me with great insights into the work. Despite being particularly uninterested in food, she made it a point to try all of my recipes and give me detailed feedback on each.

Thanks are due to my dear friend, Dr Ajanta Hazarika, for being ever willing to read whatever I wanted to sound out. I am also thankful to my friends, Nupur Sinha and Veena Chaturvedi, for having shared some of their most interesting recipes with me.

It is my mother Prema to whom I am indebted for having instilled the importance of eating right all through my growing-up years. Had it not been for her, I may never have ventured into the realm of nutrition!

My daughter Richa's critical and analytical abilities were of much use to me. With some reluctance, she served as an efficient editor of the manuscript. Many of the issues that I have faced as a mother while trying to appease the fussy eater in her have enriched my narratives.

I wish to thank the two men in my life – my husband Dinesh and my son Parth – for all the tacit ways in which they have helped me put this book together.

At the stage when I was still undecided about how to find a publisher for my book, it was Dr Sydney Rebeiro who recommended Hachette India for being an exceptional publishing house.

Vatsala, the editor of my book, has offered invaluable suggestions and comments that transformed the first draft into this book. I could not have asked for a more understanding and friendly editor.

I'd like to express my heartfelt thanks to Poulomi, Publisher at Hachette India, for agreeing to publish the book with such enthusiasm that my job became easy!

Finally, I'd like to thank all those parents and their wonderful children who have been consulting me. It is because of my interactions with all of you that I have learnt so much.